A DISCIPLE'S CHRISTOLOGY: APPRAISALS OF KRAUS'S *JESUS CHRIST OUR LORD*

RICHARD A. KAUFFMAN, EDITOR

OCCASIONAL PAPERS NO. 13

Institute of Mennonite Studies
3003 Benham Avenue
Elkhart, Indiana 46517

1989

Occasional Papers

Occasional Papers is a publication of the Institute of Mennonite Studies and authorized by the Council of Mennonite Seminaries. The four sponsoring seminaries are Eastern Mennonite Seminary (Harrisonburg, VA), Goshen Biblical Seminary and Mennonite Biblical Seminary (Elkhart, IN), and the Mennonite Brethren Biblical Seminary (Fresno, CA). The Institute of Mennonite Studies is the research agency of the Associated Mennonite Biblical Seminaries.

Occasional Papers is released several times yearly without any prescribed calendar schedule. The purpose of the *Papers* is to make various types of essays available to foster dialogue in biblical, theological and practical ministry areas and to invite critical counsel from within the Mennonite theological community. While most essays will be in finished form, some may also be in a more germinal stage--released especially for purposes of testing and receiving critical feedback. In accepting papers for publication, priority will be given to authors from the CMS institutions, the college Bible faculties in the Council of Mennonite Colleges, the associate membership of the Institute of Mennonite Studies, and students and degree alumni of the four seminaries.

Because of the limited circulation of the *Occasional Papers*, authors are free to use their material in other scholarly settings, either for oral presentation at scholarly meetings or for publication in journals with broader circulation and more official publication policies.

Orders for *Occasional Papers* should be sent to the Institute of Mennonite Studies, 3003 Benham Avenue, Elkhart, IN 46517-1999.

Copyright 1989 by Institute of Mennonite Studies, 3003 Benham Ave., Elkhart, IN 46517-1999; all rights reserved. No part of this publication may be reproduced, stored in a retrieval system, or transmitted in any form or by any means, electronic, mechanical, photocopying, or otherwise, without the prior permission of the copyright owner.

ISBN 0-936273-15-1
Printed in the U.S.A.

TABLE OF CONTENTS

PREFACE

At an earlier time and for a different purpose I commented on the ferment current in the Mennonite church on the issue of Christology. Given the fact that Mennonites tend to be a practical people not given to theological speculation, why has Christology become an issue for discussion and debate? I wondered.

Has something been lost that needs to be recovered? Are we already recovering once lost insights or gaining new ones which demand a Christology update? Has our experience changed so much that old confessions of faith seem irrelevant? Just what is the motive behind this new interest in the person and work of Christ?[1]

Whatever, the year was 1982. Since then, Christology has come even more to the surface in Mennonite thought and conversation. In part, at least, the increased attention to the subject has been precipitated by the publication of *Jesus Christ Our Lord: Christology from a Disciple's Perspective* by C. Norman Kraus (Scottdale, PA: Herald Press, 1987).

In this volume Kraus proposes a new method for doing Christology. Our understanding of Jesus Christ--his work and person--must be done from the perspective of a missionary theology. That is, it must be done within and from the particular context in which the church is bearing witness to the gospel of Jesus Christ. Further, being a Mennonite committed to the Anabaptist tradition, Kraus claims that this Christology must be a peace theology--a theology which takes seriously the claim that Jesus Christ "is our peace" (Eph. 2:14). And finally this Christology, being a disciple's theology, must be based first and foremost on the person of Jesus Christ as the norm for Christology. The implication of this is that the great ecumenical creeds of the early church aren't accepted as definitive but rather that *Gestalt* of Christ which is portrayed through the multiple witnesses to him in the New Testament.

Perhaps Kraus's approach is not entirely unique or new. At

least a part of his agenda is not unlike that proposed by contemporary theologians from other traditions. For instance, George Stroup III has proposed that, whereas Chalcedonian Christology is helpful in pointing out some of the pitfalls in our understandings of Jesus Christ, its language of natures and substance is not very meaningful to people in the twentieth century. Besides, he claims, we have a different understanding of personhood and identity than is reflected in the Chalcedonian formula. Hence, he suggests that Christology today must begin with the only narratives which we have of Jesus Christ (the New Testament rather than Chalcedon is the starting point, in other words). And our Christology must reflect a new model of personhood in which personal identity is viewed in more dynamic terms than that of the ontological language of the fifth century.[2] Kraus's approach would seem to comply with this perspective.

It is precisely this aspect of Kraus's agenda which is troubling to many: that is, the two-fold movement of going back to scripture as the primary source and norm for Christology; and then reshaping (*recontextualizing* is the jargon used) Christology using personalistic, historicist and metaphorical language rather than the ontological language of Chalcedon. Kraus's book, therefore, has provoked a debate among Mennonites which has been right below the surface for a long time now, the question of norms for theology and Christology. Is scripture the only norm for theology and Christology? How is scripture to be used in doing theology? Are creeds also normative? If so, in what way? Mennonites (including some of their Anabaptist forebears) have tended to give lip service to the conciliar creeds without ever being precise about the creeds' function or role or arbitrating their implicit authority with the more serious and foundational claim for the authority of scripture.

These methodological issues, as well as others, were dealt with at a consultation held on the campus of the Associated Mennonite Biblical Seminaries, October 8, 1988.[3] At this event Kraus himself was given two opportunities to speak formally: he gave an autobiographical introduction to his work, attempting to explain the personal and theological agenda which motivated *Jesus Christ Our Lord*; at the end of the event he responded to the papers read and the questions raised during the course of the consultation. Between his two presentations two papers were read from a biblical studies perspective and one each addressing missiological, pastoral, historical and theological issues. Although this was largely an "in house" discussion among Mennonites, three so-called "outsiders" were included as resource persons representing evangelicals, the Church of the Brethren and the Reformed tradition.

In view of the importance of Christology for Mennonites (as well as others) and more particularly because of the contribution which Kraus has made to the dialogue and ferment, the Institute of Mennonite Studies of the Associated Mennonite Biblical Seminaries decided to make the papers from this consultation more broadly accessible. Hence, they are presented here as *Occasional Paper No. 13*. In addition, we have included as an appendix book reviews of Kraus's work which have appeared in Mennonite journals and magazines. We are especially grateful for Norman Kraus's willingness to participate in this consultation and to have his presentations and those of his interlocutors included herein. Thanks also are in order to the persons who wrote these papers and to the editors of the journals and magazines whose book reviews are reprinted here with their permission.

Richard A. Kauffman, Interim Director
Institute of Mennonite Studies

ENDNOTES

1. Richard A. Kauffman, "Christology Revisited," *Gospel Herald*, vol. 75, no. 3 (January 19, 1982) 34-36.
2. George Stroup, "Christian Doctrine: Chalcedon Revisited," *Theology Today*, vol. XXXV, no. 1 (April 1978) 52-64.
3. Mennonites (or at least their Anabaptist forebears) engaged in disputations. Today we hold consultations. Call such events what you will, we can not--nor should we--dispense with theological disputes and debates. The alternative would be an insipid theology (or theologies) about which no one cares much.

CHAPTER 1
A BRIEF AUTOBIOGRAPHICAL ACCOUNT

C. Norman Kraus

I was raised a fundamental Mennonite--a premillennialist, non-conformist, faith-and-works Mennonite who attempted to hold to the "all things" of Scripture. I was baptized by George R. Brunk I and remember him well as a kindly pastor and great preacher. Now in the autumn of my life, I am still a very convinced Mennonite. However, I have seen many almost unbelievable changes in that church, and I myself am not the same cultural Mennonite I was in my youth.

Since I have written my book, *Jesus Christ Our Lord: Christology from a Disciple's Perspective*, toward the end of my career, and since it does not read quite as it might have forty years ago, perhaps it would be helpful if I shared with you a bit of my theological pilgrimage. I might call it a pilgrimage from early nineteenth-century Mennonitism through sixteenth-century Anabaptism back into twentieth-century Mennonitism.

I received my first formal theological training at Eastern Mennonite College in the classes of C. K. Lehman. There I was introduced to the theology of James Orr, B. B. Warfield, O. T. Allis, and "old" Princeton with some Mennonite reservations. I remember that the name of Barth came up briefly for criticism, but I do not even remember any mention of the name of Reinhold Niebuhr, who was then at his height. At Goshen College and Biblical Seminary I was introduced to Anabaptism by H. S. Bender, J. C. Wenger and Guy F. Hershberger. I also learned the "inductive Bible study" methodology under Howard Charles.

After teaching New Testament Greek and book studies for two years in the Goshen Biblical Seminary, I did one year of graduate study at Princeton Theological Seminary. There I discovered both American church history, and, at the other end of the historical spectrum, early church history, theology, and especially hermeneutics. While there I wrote my *Dispensationalism in America* (John Knox,

1958), and in the course of that research I discovered the roots of fundamentalism. The late Ernest Sandeen later built on this discovery and published his *The Roots of Fundamentalism.*

I became convinced that fundamentalism and Anabaptism were quite different kinds of movements, and that the great Mennonite tradition was not originally fundamentalist as John Horsch had argued earlier in this century. That year at Princeton (1953-54) I decided that rather than continuing the study of sixteenth-century Anabaptism God was calling me to help the Mennonite Church understand its twentieth-century American environment and its own self-identity in that setting. (At that point we were not even offering courses in American church history in our seminary!)

Again after a number of years of teaching at Goshen College I went to Duke University to finish my doctoral training. Here I surveyed the American theological tradition in greater detail from the Puritans and Jonathan Edwards to the Niebuhrs and Tillich. I did my dissertation research on B. B. Warfield, William Adams Brown, and Gerald Birney Smith--an orthodox Calvinist, a middle of the road liberal, and a radical modernist.

During this study I discovered that there was a broad conservative middle in American and English theology that had been largely overlooked in the heat of the modernist-fundamentalist debate. There were men like A. H. Strong, E. Y. Mullins, and James Orr who had even written articles for the first volume of *The Fundamentals.* And in England there were men like P. T. Forsyth and James Denny who were truly conservative and evangelical but not fundamentalist. I found this theological alternative very attractive.

I discovered that the categories of "liberal" and "fundamentalist" were much too restricted to understand the great theological tradition of the church. Although I did not agree entirely with Karl Barth or Emil Brunner, I could see that they were wrongly classified as "new liberals" by persons like Cornelius Van Til. And I became increasingly convinced that Anabaptist-Mennonite theological positions needed a classification of their own. *Mennonites were neither liberals nor fundamentalists.* They had a biblical tradition of their own, and I felt that they could and should speak to the issues raised by liberalism from the perspective of their own tradition rather than to simply identify themselves as "fundamentalists plus."

Back at Goshen College I taught courses in Bible, Protestant church history and theology, and a course called "The Christian Faith." I began to draw out the differences between the Anabaptist-Mennonite and the classical Protestant traditions. Although Robert Friedmann's contrast between Pietism and Anabaptism seemed too sharp (see *Mennonite Piety through the Centuries,* 1949), I was convinced that our tradition represents a third alternative. Indeed, Walter Klaassen and I talked about this some years before he published his little classic, *Anabaptism: Neither Catholic Nor Protestant* (1973).

I suppose that it was inevitable that I would often be labeled "liberal" since I criticized fundamentalism as well as liberalism. Those on the fundamentalist right in our circles thought that I was much harder on fundamentalism than liberalism. And since I no longer espoused the inerrancy theory and the hermeneutic that accompanied it, they were sure that I was liberal! But if in fact I was more openly critical of fundamentalism, it was because I saw it as a much greater immediate threat to twentieth-century American Mennonites. Up until the sixties our brush with liberalism had made little impact. The danger of Mennonites selling out to acculturated American fundamentalism seemed much more serious to me. I remember once remarking to the late John E. Lapp, who represented much of the best in our tradition, that I thought some of us "young bucks" and he had more in common than either of us had in common with our fundamentalistically inclined brothers and sisters.

Now at this point (1988) I think that the liberal, humanist threat is much greater in the Mennonite circles than it was earlier, and the fundamentalist threat is not much diminished. Indeed, in my pessimistic moments I sometimes think that it is the very pervasiveness of fundamentalism among us that prompts the liberal reaction. In any case, we are now obliged to guard ourselves on both sides. My book, *Jesus Christ Our Lord*, is an attempt to offer an alternative theological hermeneutic which, I am convinced, is both more biblical than either pole of Protestant theology and therefore more Anabaptist.

Some developing theological convictions

Over the years I have become increasingly aware that the implications of the Anabaptists' dissent were theologically more radical than we had at first interpreted them. The Lutheran and Reformed theologians did not always understand what the Anabaptists were trying to say and therefore sometimes raised the wrong issues. They were correct, however, in their suspicions that not only medieval church tradition but also the tradition from Nicea through Augustine was being challenged.

In twentieth century Mennonite interpretations of Anabaptism this theological radicality was muted. At a time in the American experience when we were attempting to find our place in the denominational pattern we tended to emphasize the essential orthodoxy of the Anabaptists. We even implied that the "biblical" Anabaptists--the true ancestors of the modern Mennonites--would fit into the contemporary free church denominational pattern. The radicality of the original Anabaptists was to be understood in ethical and social-political terms, not theological terms.

Further, I became aware that *Christ* and not the Bible, not even the New Testament as such, functioned as the formal theological authority for most Anabaptists. They did, of course, have their share of literalists, and the humanist's watchword, *ad fontes*, gave the Bible new centrality and authority over tradition. But if we ask what gave Scripture its authority for them, and what was the hermeneutical norm for distinguishing between the relative authority of Old and New Testaments, the answer is Christ to whom it bears witness. To use a term which became common parlance in the third and fourth generation of post-Reformation theology, the Bible was not God's word because it is "inerrant" but because it bears authentic witness to Jesus as the Christ--his life, teachings, death and resurrection.

Second, I became convinced that the Mennonite "peace position" cannot be adequately developed under the rubric of Luther's "two kingdoms" theory. (This concept is also implicit in Calvinistic orthodoxy although with different conclusions for the church's involvement in society and politics.) John H. Yoder has worked extensively with this question and has suggested the "middle axiom" as a way of applying Christ's kingship to our historical social existence.

What we generally have not noted in Mennonite circles is that the two kingdom schema--temporal-spiritual, public-private, social-individual--with its attending secular and religious vocations is the logical counterpart of other theological definitions. It parallels the definition of Christ's "human *and* divine" natures, of God's moral nature characterized as *both* justice *and* love, and his dealing with humankind under *both* law *and* grace.

In each case these contrasting characteristics stand in tension with each other and are resolved by "paradox." In Lutheran theology this paradox in the Christian life is spelled out under the rubric of "justification"--*simul iustus et peccator*. The Anabaptist position on the other hand emphasized reconciliation, transformation, and peace which by implication changed the nature of these theological "both/and" definitions. (For example, Menno's "heavenly flesh of Christ," Marpeck's "godded humanity" of Christ, and Denck's reevaluation of love and justice in God's character are all attempts to overcome the "both/and" paradox which seemed to allow Christians to be justified *in* their sin.)

Third, by the mid-seventies I became convinced through my experiences in Asia that the proper missiological approach is to begin in each cultural context with a *pre-dogmatic biblical picture of Jesus as the Christ.* (This is what I understand Fr. Avery Dulles to mean by "from below," i.e., not to begin with dogmatic definitions. My concern is not the same as that of Ritschl and liberal theology although one must recognize him as the first to use the term.) I am concerned that the missionary message begin with the inspired apostolic witness *(kerygma)* and build a contextual theological interpretation. In that process, of course, comparative studies from the church's experience in history and other cultures should come into full play. A major continuing role for the western missionary lies in helping the first generation church to understand the significance of this historical experience of the church ecumenical in the development of its own theology.

I am convinced that to be true to the New Testament, theology must be primarily missionary theology, i.e., theology for discipling the people of the world's cultures. That means in the first instance that the goal of theologizing is to bring our own lives under the transforming discipline of Christ. Then from the perspective of a disciple we share with others the original experience of those who walked with him in the flesh.

I have been criticized by some for not speaking more directly to the question, "Why Christ rather than some other great religious figure?" My answer is that such an answer can be given only as authentic witness to the self-revelation of God in Jesus. It cannot ultimately be given in the analytic of comparative religions; not in apologetic or polemical theological confrontation; and certainly not by a dialogue which assumes the relativity of Christ among the world's religious leaders. An authentic witness must include both proclamation of the apostolic Christ and a demonstration of his power in the life of individuals and the church.

My Asia experiences beginning in 1966 also confirmed my earlier discovery that language has multiple uses. Already in the early fifties I had read Susanne K. Langer's *Philosophy in a New Key.* Then later I dipped into the dialogue which was going on between the philosophers of Logical Positivism and British theologians. It was in this dialogue that the many functions of language were analyzed. In my Asia and Africa experience I found that language does indeed play different roles in different cultures. This opened up anew the question of its uses in the Bible which was inspired and written in an ancient west Asian culture. Our modern western empirical bias has often blinded us to the subtle variations and symbolism in the eastern cultures!

I hope that this will give some insight into my frame of mind and purpose for writing *Jesus Christ our Lord: Theology from a Disciple's Perspective.* I have long intended to write a theology, but I was aware of how much one needs to understand of the history of theology, and the biblical disciplines, so I delayed the process. My mission in Japan gave me a congenial setting and strong motivation. My dominant concern was to help these new, but sophisticated Christians understand the gospel. And a continuous class of students intent on covering the whole field of theology provided an ideal setting.

CHAPTER 2
BIBLICAL CONSIDERATIONS

Dorothy Jean Weaver

Jesus Christ Our Lord: Christology from a Disciple's Perspective is a book which has long been waiting to be written. Here Kraus offers to the world of Anabaptist scholarship--and beyond that to the broader world of theological scholarship--a cogent and compelling Anabaptist formulation of the christological question, the question concerning the identity and significance of Jesus of Nazareth.

Speaking broadly, this book accomplishes two aims. First, in laying out a systematic christological statement from an Anabaptist perspective this book points backward to the theoretical (read "biblical") framework upon which Anabaptist treatments of salvation, discipleship, and ethics have been built. Kraus's book, therefore, lays bare the biblical underpinnings of the Anabaptist approach to soteriology, ecclesiology and ethics.

Second, this book gathers the evidence from the biblical witness concerning Jesus of Nazareth into a creative and challenging reformulation of the christological question itself. In this way Kraus points forward from an Anabaptist understanding of the biblical texts in their multiplicity to the systematic christological statement which emerges from such an understanding of the texts.

My task within this paper is to examine Kraus's book from the standpoint of the first of these concerns, the concern with the biblical texts and their witness to Jesus of Nazareth. I will group my comments into three major sections: (1) overall reflections on Kraus's aims, presuppositions, and methodology; (2) overall reflections on Kraus's thesis; (3) specific questions concerning Kraus's methodology and substance.

Overall reflections on Kraus's aims, presuppositions, methodology

As a biblical scholar operating out of an Anabaptist frame of reference, I find *Jesus Christ Our Lord* book to be not only refreshing in its outlook, but immensely stimulating as well. The distinctive shape of Kraus's christology and, as I see it, the significant strengths of this work can be seen from the convergence of a variety of perspectives.

In the first place, Kraus makes it clear that his christological reflection takes place not in the service of the world of academia and its academic theories, but rather in the service of "the disciple church" and its "life and work" (p. 16). As Kraus puts it, "We need a theological description that will . . . give us a clue to our own self-understanding as followers of Christ and guide us into a relevant discipleship (pp. 29-30)."[1] While Kraus is by no means anti-academic, his scholarship answers above all to the church and not to the academy. This praxis-oriented concern corresponds in a fundamental way not only to the Anabaptist thought world out of which Kraus comes but also to the clearly pastoral/practical concerns of the New Testament writers themselves. And from this standpoint his approach as a whole is distinctly biblical.

Secondly, Kraus positions himself centrally and solidly on the question of the authority and interpretation of Scripture. On the one hand he distinguishes himself from the position widely represented within Evangelicalism "that the whole New Testament is a verbally inspired, inerrant record . . . [which is] to be understood as literal history (p. 30)." On the other hand he sets himself apart from the "liberal rationalistic" approach reflected most prominently in the work of Rudolf Bultmann, an approach which "insist[s] on human reason as the final norm for interpreting the Bible" (p. 30) and holds that the New Testament texts "must be *demythologized* for our use today" (p. 31, n. 6). In line with his primary concern for the "disciple church" Kraus suggests that "both of these *rationalistic* systems have failed for the same reason: they have tried to substitute theoretical justification of logical statements for an authentic practical response of the church to Jesus Christ as *Lord*" (p. 33).

In response to these opposing rationalistic systems Kraus then identifies his own position as follows: "We shall begin, therefore, with the acceptance of the New Testament as the reliable witness to the continuity and historical concurrance [sic] between the earthly Jesus and the church's experience of the risen Christ" (p. 34). This position allows Kraus to draw on the New Testament texts unhesitatingly and to treat them with utmost seriousness, while at the same time it frees him from the necessity of viewing these texts anachronistically as contemporary "scientific" or "historical" writings. Growing out of this approach to the New Testament as a "reliable witness" to the Christ event are two correlates. On the one hand, Kraus adopts a developmental approach to Christology ("Christology from below," pp. 36, 49, 57). Such an approach allows the christological portrait of Jesus of Nazareth to emerge inductively from the study of the New Testament writings: "We begin with Jesus of Nazareth as experienced personal reality and ask who this Jesus is. We do not begin with later philosophical definitions and assumptions . . . and then read the New Testament data in light of these assumptions" (p. 57). In short, this approach attempts to do justice to the process through which the earliest Christians themselves came to discover the significance of Jesus of Nazareth, a process which did not occur suddenly and systematically but rather slowly and incrementally.

In line with this developmental approach Kraus likewise adopts a metaphorical approach to the christological portrait of Jesus which emerges from the New Testament writings. Speaking broadly, this approach recognizes that "Jesus himself is the metaphor of God. He is the 'Word of God' and the 'Event' of salvation in which God is present to us in our historical existence" (p. 57). Speaking more specifically, this approach recognizes the broad range of metaphors which the New Testament writers pull into service to describe the significance of Jesus of Nazareth;[2] and it implicitly rejects any attempt to undercut this fundamental diversity of christological language through the establishment of "simple rational definitions."[3] This approach thus recognizes that christological formulations are precisely not "laws of the universe" but rather "confessions of faith," attempts to describe by human analogies the significance of God's inbreaking into human history in the person of Jesus of Nazareth.

Third, Kraus defines his task in rigorously "christocentric" fashion. In contrast to systematic theologians who take their point of departure from Trinitarian understandings, Kraus raises the "intriguing possibility" (p. 18) that all systematic theologies, to the extent to which they claim to be "authentically Christian," should move out from a christological center and beginning point. In his words (p. 18),

> why not begin with an account of Jesus as "the Christ of God" and discuss the whole range of theological questions in relation to the self-revelation of God in him? Why not make explicit what is formally implicit in all authentically Christian theologies? Why, for example, should we assume that the Trinitarian principle is prior to and more comprehensive than the christological principle? To begin with Jesus as the Christ does not necessarily imply a sectarian or

non-Trinitarian position. After all, in the historical development of theology, it was the orthodox Christology of the
third and fourth centuries which necessitated a doctrine of
the Trinity.[4]

Here again, Kraus's approach shows itself to be strongly biblical. There seems little room to debate the notion that all of the New
Testament writers are doing exactly what Kraus is proposing,
namely, rethinking their entire *theological* framework in the light of
the *christological* event which has taken place in the life, death, and
resurrection of Jesus of Nazareth.[5] To carry their "inchoate
Christologies" (p. 35) forward into a "systematic christology" is accordingly to follow their fundamental procedure to its natural conclusion.

Fourth, in line with the above concerns Kraus establishes the
ultimate goal of his Christology as missiological in character. As he
phrases it (p. 38), "theology is concerned precisely with the mission
of the church in the world . . . because the mission of the church is
theological." Elsewhere (p. 19) he identifies "the existential missionary reason" for setting forth his Christology:

> The first serious theological question I was asked after we
> arrived in Hokkaido, Japan, in 1981 was "Why did Jesus
> have to die?" This volume has grown out of extended dis-
> cussion of the biblical answer to that question in the
> Japanese context as well as reflection upon my previous
> thirty years of reading and teaching [in an American set-
> ting].

This focus once again marks Kraus's work as strongly biblical in
its approach. As was the case with the christocentric approach
described above, there seems little room to debate the notion that
the New Testament documents are intensely "missionary" in their
thrust. If they are, in fact, addressed to the "already converted," they
nevertheless have as one of their central intentions that of energizing
believers to carry "the Good News of Jesus Christ" to those who are
not yet among the family of faith.[6]

From a New Testament standpoint, therefore, the above
emphases distinguish Kraus's book as solidly biblical in its approach.
The New Testament writings clearly reflect not only the same
concerns--pastoral/practical, christological, and missiological--which
give focus to Kraus's work but also the developmental process and
the metaphorical approach to which Kraus bears witness. Kraus's
work thus represents a significant attempt to build a Christology not

deductively--i.e., in line with any external dogmatic statements or philosophical frameworks brought to the biblical texts and super-imposed on them--but rather *inductively*--in line with those same concerns which compelled the New Testament writers themselves to take pen in hand.[7]

Overall reflections on Kraus's thesis

Without any question the major contribution of Kraus's book emerges from the radically "christocentric" fashion in which he reads the New Testament and out of which he constructs his christology. Rather than subordinating New Testament *christological* for-mulations to an already established *theological* framework, his meth-odology moves in reverse fashion from its beginning point in the New Testament portrait of Jesus of Nazareth to consequent conclu-sions about the nature of God and of God's relationship to humankind. In other words, it is not what we already know about the nature of God which explains to us who Jesus is, but what we know about Jesus of Nazareth which tells us who God is.

The beauty and the radicality of this approach lie in its utter simplicity. To start with the premise that it is Jesus of Nazareth who shows us the nature of God and of God's dealings with humankind is to chart a straight path through a vast wilderness of theological and ethical issues. If Jesus of Nazareth is truly the one who shows us the nature of God, then the beginning point for our theologizing must lie in our examination of the life, death, and resurrection of this Jesus and nowhere else. And when we take the New Testament portrayal of Jesus of Nazareth as the basis for our understanding of God, we discover a God whose nature is as unexpected as it is evident:

> His Law is the law of love. His power, authority, and judg-ment are exercised among us like Jesus' power, authority, and judgment were expressed. God, our Savior takes the form of a servant. He comes as one of the disinherited and oppressed. His kingly crown is made of thorns. He dies as a criminal executed on a cross because the political and reli-gious powers judge that that is the only way the nation can be saved. But because he is the God of life he rises from his grave in order to continue his work as Savior-Servant of the universe. And this is not one small link in the chain of his-tory. It *is* the chain. This *is* the pattern, the *Gestalt* or form, that God takes in relation to us. (p. 103)

Kraus's christocentric approach thus allows us to see clearly and unambiguously that *according to the New Testament witness* it is above all suffering and persisting love (and not therefore retributive justice) which defines the character of God. And this understanding, in turn, alters the entire basis for Christian theology. As Kraus points out (p. 17):

> Protestant orthodoxy has from the beginning interpreted the cross in a way that justifies religious imperialism and the use of violence to achieve the ends of God's kingdom. This is not simply the interpretation of a few key passages which a peace theology might challenge. It involves the fundamental definitions of love and justice, the nature of the biblical witness and authority, and the meaning of incarnation itself.

The major contribution of Kraus's book, therefore, lies in the fact that it redefines the terms which provide the basic language for Christian theologizing and reshapes the framework within which Christian theology takes place and does so *on the basis of the New Testament witness itself.*[8] Kraus here offers us a solidly biblical "peace theology" which "undergird[s] and . . . explain[s] the implications of the cross and resurrection as God's way of dealing with evil" (p. 17); and for this contribution we can be immensely grateful.

Specific questions concerning Kraus's methodology and substance

While I am in broad agreement with Kraus's presuppositions, methodology, and conclusions, I nevertheless wish to raise a variety of questions either for clarification or for further discussion. I have categorized these questions according to type.

Questions concerning definitions:

1. Kraus's language concerning "a/the historical Jesus" is somewhat confusing. Compare page 86 ("Neither can a scientific reconstruction of the 'historical Jesus' replace the apostolic witness.") with page 90 ("First, a historical resurrection is the ratification of a historical Jesus of Nazareth as the servant of Yahweh"). How is the word "historical" to be defined? Must it be given two different definitions? If so, what are they?
2. How are the terms "warrior-martyr" (pp. 135-137) and "radical-martyr" (p. 146) to be understood? In what sense is the

"messianic warrior" to be understood as a "martyr"? As one who *gives his life* in the cause of God's retributive justice? As one who *witnesses to* God's retributive justice? And to what does the term "radical martyr" point? Does "martyr" have the same meaning here as in the term "warrior-martyr"? In what sense does the term "radical" stand in contrast to the term "warrior"?

Issues which need further exegetical support:

1. The discussion (p. 140) concerning the mission of Jesus' disciples ("A third possibility exists . . .") begs for exegetical support. Kraus first notes, "Here we must be precise in our statement of [Jesus'] commission." But he then goes on to make a variety of statements concerning that mission, none of which is backed up by a single scriptural reference. While he does point the reader to a lengthier treatment of the topic in his book *The Authentic Witness* (p. 141, n. 5), that indication alone is hardly sufficient for the present context.

2. There is likewise need for further exegetical support in the discussion (p. 214) of "shame" as a biblical concept. The two paragraphs in which Kraus treats this issue are strikingly short on scriptural references and scarcely provide the basis which he needs for his overall thesis concerning the significance of "shame." I do not question that the exegetical support may exist, but I do wish to see that support laid out at greater length and in greater detail.

Questions concerning methodology:

1. In light of the fact that one of Kraus's major methodological aims is to question the adequacy of "metaphysical conceptualization" as a basis for theological analogy (pp. 46-48), it is unclear to me why he then brings "ontological" language back into service to describe the nature of sin: "First, we must understand that guilt is not created by law or ultimately defined by it. Guilt is ontological, not merely legal" (p. 224).

2. I am uneasy with the method by which Kraus constructs his *Gestalt* of Jesus of Nazareth. On the one hand Kraus recognizes (p. 26) that there are "a number of different pictures of Jesus" in the Gospels and "a multiplicity of Christ images and metaphors" in the epistles; and he asks the question, "Which one shall we use?" But rather than laying out these "different pictures" and "multiple images" in their own right (Gospel by Gospel or epistle by epistle) and allowing them to enter into genuine dialogue with each other, Kraus immediately sets out to piece the various pictures into a single

and internally consistent collage which he labels his "*Gestalt*." My question has less to do with the validity of Kraus's final product, his *Gestalt*, than with the unrealistically smooth transition from "different pictures" and "multiple images" to that final product. Does Kraus's approach do justice to the unmistakable and energetic dialogue represented within the New Testament documents concerning the significance of Jesus of Nazareth? Would it not be of the essence in a work such as this to document the christological dialogue reflected in the New Testament writings *before* submerging the differences into a single, internally consistent *Gestalt*?[9]

Questions concerning Kraus's exegetical work:

1. I find Kraus's discussion (pp. 76-77) of the "historicity of the virgin birth" somewhat problematic. On the one hand Kraus apparently concurs with the statement of J. C. Wenger (p. 77, n. 17) that "the miracle of incarnation is of the same order as that of creation, and the accounts of Jesus' conception have the same 'highly poetic character.'" On the other hand Kraus states that "it is highly unlikely that the original writers intended a literalistic interpretation such as that upon which modern science insists" (p. 76). What Kraus appears to overlook in his analysis is that the "highly poetic" creation accounts to which Wenger refers represent no less than the best informed "science" of the day. If an analogy is to be drawn from the creation accounts to the virgin birth accounts, it points *toward* rather than *away from* the "literalistic interpretation" (*on the part of the original writers*) which Kraus considers "highly unlikely." (It is obviously a valid question, but one of the *second order*, to ask how *we* relate to the [tenth century B.C.] "scientific" account of creation and the [first century A.D.] "scientific" account of the virgin birth.)

2. A larger exegetical question has to do with Kraus's apparent avoidance of the language and imagery of judgment within the sayings traditions of the Gospels. In his discussion of the basis of Jesus' authority (p. 146) Kraus states categorically that Jesus "did not threaten the people with God's punitive power which, like Elijah of old, he might have commanded." While Kraus further defines this "threat of punitive power" as the "threat of violence" (presumably on the part of Jesus himself), Kraus's categorical statement is hardly an accurate reflection of the evidence. If we are to credit the authenticity of the sayings traditions (which Kraus clearly does), there is within the teachings of Jesus a striking emphasis on eschatological judgment which will separate the "wheat" from the "chaff," sort out the "bad fish" from the "good fish," separate the "goats" from the "sheep," etc.[10] There can be no question that Jesus

(along with his contemporaries) viewed this coming judgment as the action of God and no one else. It is difficult, therefore, to know how else to describe such texts than as "appeals to God's punitive power," regardless of the difficulty which such appeals may provide for us. In all events, it is a striking omission on the part of Kraus to largely disregard this major body of material in creating his *Gestalt* of Jesus of Nazareth.

3. A closely related question has to do with Kraus's treatment of the apocalyptic material outside of the sayings traditions of the Gospels (primarily Revelation). While Kraus does not overlook this material (pp. 198-200; cf. pp. 153-154), he clearly views it as second-rate christologizing by comparison to the essentially Pauline christological imagery with which he contrasts it (pp. 200-201). In Kraus's words, "At best the apocalyptic imagery is esoteric and ambiguous, and it is of limited use in conveying the message of God's salvation through Christ" (p. 199). But does Kraus in fact do justice to New Testament apocalyptic by such a statement? It would appear that Kraus's difficulty with the apocalyptic language of the sayings traditions on the one hand and the apocalyptic imagery and genre of Revelation on the other stem from the same source. And the question which this observation raises is whether Kraus--in downplaying or largely ignoring the abundance of apocalyptic imagery within the New Testament--has created an adequate *Gestalt* of Jesus of Nazareth.

4. A different set of questions relates to Kraus's description of "the role of Jesus Christ in the formation of humankind into God's image" (p. 196). On page 73 Kraus states that Paul "cites Jesus as our *exemplar*, which means more than following his moral example to the best of our ability. We are to have his 'mind'and to be conformed to his image" (Phil. 2:2,5; 2 Cor. 3:18; Eph. 2:11-19). But, as he concludes, "this does not mean that we are to be superhuman; rather, we are to emulate his humanity." In similar fashion Kraus speaks of the "personal-social dynamic (indicated in a variety of New Testament texts cited) in which Christ is the paradigm, exemplar, or role model who stimulates, trains, and encourages us to share his achievement of the image of God" (p. 197). My question is whether Kraus has recognized sufficiently the ubiquitous motif of "power/empowerment" which runs throughout the New Testament documents, gospels and epistles alike. Is "emulation" on our part or "stimulation" on Christ's part an adequate replacement for the concepts of "empowerment" and "empowering?" Is this shift "substantial" or "semantic"?

Endnotes

1. Cf. Kraus's explanation (pp. 36-37): "We have said that Christology is theology and have noted the need for a coherent theological portrait of Jesus. Does that mean that we are going to speculate, theorize, and dogmatize about Jesus? Should we not be more concerned to *experience* Jesus as Christ, proclaim him as Savior, and follow him as Lord? Would it not be more useful to share the personal stories of our experience with Christ? Is not the experience itself theological, thus giving the stories the character of theology? After all, life is more than logic; indeed, logic is often too narrow for life's realities. What does a theoretical analysis of Jesus' identity have to do with practical Christianity? I am convinced that it is vitally related to each of the above-mentioned practical areas. In a word, it is *theory in the service of practice*." Stated more succinctly, Kraus's thesis reads (p. 38): "*Faith* is a conviction and trust based upon hearing the word about Jesus as the Christ and experiencing it as 'the power of God for salvation' (Rom. 1:16-17). And *theology* is our attempt to express the meaning and implications of this experience for our life in the world."

2. See, for example, Kraus's discussions on pp. 127-32 and 171-201.

3. As Kraus observes (p. 173), "The Bible, as we have noted, uses a number of metaphors rather than a simple rational definition to describe God's salvation. . . . Furthermore, the Bible does not standardize the metaphors. Different writers seem to prefer different metaphors. For these reasons the theological task calls for classification and assigning of interpretative priorities as well as simple explanation of the metaphors."

4. Kraus then follows through in consistent fashion with this christocentric focus. Reflective of this overall approach is his statement (p. 103) with reference to the incarnation: "It is not that the God of Moses--the Creator, Law-giver and Judge (i.e., God, the Omnipotent and Transcendent One)--who is already well-known humbles himself temporarily to become our servant and savior in Jesus who is his Son. Rather, we are saying that the God who at best was dimly and inadequately known through creation and law reveals the fuller dimensions of his character to us in Jesus."

5. See, for example, such diverse texts as Hebrews 1:1-2, Luke 24:13-35, and the so-called "formula quotations" of the Gospel of Matthew (1:22, 2:15, etc.).

6. See, for example, Romans 1:1-6, 2 Corinthians 6:18-20, Matthew 28:16-20, Acts 1:8.

7. Kraus does not operate in a vacuum, to be sure. His appropriation of "historical" and "personal" language--rather than the language of "metaphysics" and "ontology"--to talk about the significance of Jesus of Nazareth does in fact supply a theoretical framework within which Kraus operates. Nevertheless, it is evident that Kraus has chosen this language precisely because this is the language which, he believes, reflects most adequately the self-understandings of the biblical texts themselves (see p. 58, for example). This stands therefore in marked contrast to the

approach of Bultmann, who consciously "demythologizes" the self-understandings of the biblical texts before he finds it possible to appropriate the texts.

8. This refers as well to the language used as the basis for theological analogy (see n. 7 above). Kraus's work in replacing the language of "metaphysics" and "ontology" with "historical" and "personal" language is scarcely less significant a contribution than his rigorously "christocentric" approach.

9. Kraus does allow the texts to engage in dialogue with each other at a few places (pp. 198-201 on eschatology; p. 241, n. 11 on social practices in the early churches); but this sort of dialogue is disappointingly scarce in Kraus's work overall.

10. See, for example, such representative examples as the following Matthean texts: 8:11-12; 10:14-15; 12:31-32, 36-37; 13:24-30, 36-43, 47-50; 16:24-28; 18:23-35; 21:33-46; 22:1-14; 24:36-44, 45-51; 25:1-13, 14-30, 31-46.

CHAPTER 3
CHRISTOLOGY AND CONTEXTUALIZATION

Grant R. Osborne

The development of a modern Christology is indeed a daunting task, especially in light of the fact that the discipline is undergoing methodological controversy. Gerald O'Collins (1983:5-12, see bibliography appended to this chapter) notes six areas in which the traditional approach is being rethought: (1) The Christology "from above" (the Chalcedonian creed centering upon Jesus' divinity) is being challenged by a Christology from below (Jesus' genuine humanity); the two must be balanced. (2) The incarnation-centered christology of the past is being replaced by an Easter-centered approach as the true starting point. (3) The Chalcedonian affirmation of "two natures in one person" is said to submerge the human within the divine; modern christologies as a result seek to be more aware of the intersubjectivity and self-awareness of Jesus' personhood. (4) Recent attempts seek a more sophisticated differentiation between the facts (e.g. Jesus' birth and death) and faith-statements (e.g. the virgin birth or substitutionary atonement) in New Testament christological confession. (5) The ministry of Jesus (e.g. his miracles and sayings) is becoming predominant in the development of early Christology. (6) The separation between Jesus' person (Christology) and work (soteriology) is no longer considered viable. Finally, I would add to O'Collins' list a seventh tendency: the desire to contextualize a modern Christology in terms of its relevance for our day. The desire is for an indigenized theology which speaks to modern needs rather than to a merely theoretical model which describes the confession of the past.

C. Norman Kraus's *Jesus Christ Our Lord* admirably takes its place within the list of modern Christologies. Consciously taking a confessional stance (as an Anabaptist Christology) and in constant dialogue with a contextual situation (Japanese religion), this work forges bold new paths as it blends Christology, soteriology, and ecclesiology under the rubric of the lordship of Jesus within the discipleship tradition of Anabaptist theology. As one who is currently working in the field of biblical hermeneutics, I am impressed with the insight and depth of this work.

The task of developing a Christology according to hermeneutical guidelines is indeed a daunting task. The first step is to decide upon a starting point. Kraus discusses this in his first two chapters, particularly under "normative patterns" (pp. 30-34) and "modal options" (pp. 44-52). The response to Bultmann's denial of a historical model is very well done, as is the conscious missiological thrust of the approach, centering upon "theory in the service of practice" (p. 37). Yet at the same time one could have wished Professor Kraus had greater access to the vast amount of recent work on Christology,[1] for many areas are left uncovered. For instance, the discussion has moved somewhat beyond Bultmann to the historicism of Pannenberg, the eschatological system of Moltmann, the religio-historical approach of Dunn, the sacramental theology of Schillebeeckx, and the use of process theology, wisdom categories, new sociological techniques, and liberation theology to redefine the parameters of christological discussion.[2] While Kraus interacts with many of these scholars, the schools of thought they represent are not given sufficient attention. Of particular interest for the Japanese situation with its ongoing debate between left and right political camps would be the liberation and materialist christologies of Sobrino and Belo.[3] While Sobrino is mentioned (pp. 28-29), it would have been good to add this and other modern systems to the list of "modal options" (pp. 44f.).

One of the most disquieting aspects of this book occurs right here in chapters four and five, centering upon the Johannine concept of Jesus as the logos (pp. 97-105). There Kraus views the Chalcedonian concept of pre-existence and incarnation as a Greek interpretation of the text which will not bear that weight. Kraus argues that a Hebrew rather than a Greek approach separates the word of God from Jesus the person. Thereby the logos teaching of John 1:1-18 expresses "the embodiment of the pre-existent word in the earthly Jesus" (p. 100) and "does not mean that Jesus existed before his birth" (p. 105). This must be strongly challenged from an exegetical standpoint. First, all major commentators of John's gospel would concur, and here I looked through about a dozen of them, especially Raymond E. Brown's massive *Anchor Bible Commentary*, and Rudolf Schnackenberg's three volume work. Schnackenberg himself stresses the personal nature of the logos; all the major commentators as well speak clearly of the personal unity between the logos and Jesus and of the literal pre-existence of Jesus taught in the text. James Dunn in his *Christology in the Making*, with whom Kraus himself says he is largely in agreement, declares unequivocally that in John's prologue it is "beyond dispute, [that] the word is pre-existent and Christ is the pre-existent word incarnate."

Very often Kraus almost does a Moltmann-type dichotomizing between the logos and Jesus similar to that which Moltmann does with the Son of man, Jesus. Neither interpretation can be maintained exegetically. John 1:1,14 identifies Jesus clearly with the logos as both the word become flesh and the word which was God. In contrast, Kraus's thought is an almost adoptionistic view of the logos placed into the man of Jesus by God. The biblical data in my opinion does not support such a conclusion and this is a very grave misgiving at this particular point and obviously the most serious issue in the book.

The "starting point" for Christology should certainly be the "narrative Christology" of the Gospels. The old method of studying the titles for Jesus in the New Testament has clearly been replaced by a more responsible approach which allows the developing theology of the early church to speak for itself. Kraus correctly perceives this when he notes the "multidimensional" (pp. 52f.) and "metaphorical" (pp. 56f.) nature of a historical approach to christology. In this light Ben Meyer and Royce Gruenler[4] argue that the self-consciousness of Jesus himself provides the proper starting point for discussion. The so-called "shifting sands" of historical opinion do not provide an insurmountable barrier to the diachronic development of the early Church's Christology, and therefore it is an absolute necessity to study Jesus' own understanding as the foundation of later thinking.[5] Thus we begin with two related ideas, Jesus' sense of unique filial sonship and that of Christus Victor. The former is based on the "Abba" title and the divine testimony at the baptism and transfiguration (Mk. 1:11, 9:7 and parallels), the other with Jesus' exorcisms seen as part of the cosmic conflict and defeat of the demonic realm (Mk. 3:27 and parallels). The third major emphasis coming from Jesus' own understanding is his redemptive purpose, exemplified not only in the Pauline literature but also in the words of institution (Mk. 14:24 and parallels) and in the narrative development of Jesus as the agent of divine reconciliation and forgiveness.[6]

It is the Pauline literature of course which is the primary source of christological material. Kraus does an excellent job of blending Paul with the Gospels and of recognizing both diachronic and synchronic factors in developing his concept of the divine and human in the God-man, Christ Jesus. Especially relevant was the section on Jesus as the "hermeneutical norm" (pp. 82f.) for both testaments and for Christian experience as a whole. He correctly realizes that it is only in light of these larger realities that the titles of Christ can be discussed (pp. 91f.). Yet the major contribution of this central section lies in the recognition that the christological affirmations of the New Testament were not philosophical definitions but were confessional and missiological at the core. This work is methodologically very sophisticated in its understanding of biblical language and its relation to categories of Jesus' personhood. While I would not personally see so great a dichotomy between the rational analogy of being exemplified in the Chalcedonian creed and the "analogy of personal knowledge" (an identity of essence between Father and Son as in Pannenberg, cf. pp. 112-117) adopted by Kraus, I applaud the effort to make sense out of one of the most difficult theological concepts in Christian theology.

The heart of the contribution of Anabaptist thinking to Christology is section two on the "mission" of Jesus. Rejecting the normal Protestant teaching regarding Jesus as priest (the soteriological side), Kraus stresses Jesus as king (lordship). His discussion of the New Testament emphasis rightly begins with the Gospels seen as historical statements in juxtaposition with Jewish expectations (ch. 7). Jesus' rejection of the warrior-Messiah (political) model and his announcement of the kingdom (spiritual) model is interpreted as an act of *agape*. Here Kraus would have been aided greatly by turning to biblical theology, particularly the individual theologies of the four Gospels. The centrality of the kingly portrait in Matthew and Mark, of lordship in Luke, and the "glory" theme of John would have provided depth and further corroboration of the arguments therein. For instance, in Matthew and John the cross becomes Jesus' throne, and he enters his messianic office through suffering. This would have provided an invaluable transition to chapter eight on the theodicy of the cross. Moreover, historically the Gospels are the fourth level of christological development after Jesus, the New Testament creeds (e.g. Phil. 2:5-11, Rom. 1:3-4), and the epistles. Therefore they should have been explored more carefully.

The chapters exploring the soteriological dimensions of Jesus' mission are another major contribution of this book. I particularly enjoyed the chapter on theodicy, demonstrating how the cross was the New Testament replacement for the Old Testament's Law in order to defend the justice and goodness of God in light of the world and system which he has created. As an act of *agape* the cross proves that God has both entered the world of suffering and provided the solution for the world of sin.

However, chapters 10-11 on "Metaphors of Salvation" and "Salvation as Renewal of the Image of God," while well written, clearly go beyond a book on Christology into soteriology proper. It would have been better to dig more deeply into the christological side of the doctrine of salvation. The discussion of salvific metaphors is quite controversial, centering as it does upon the meaning of justification and the demonic conflict. The classical Protestant definition of "justification" involves the forensic idea of "declared righteous" on the basis of the substitutionary atonement wrought by Christ.[7] This idea is stressed also in the ransom idea behind "redemption" terminology, as Jesus' "blood" sets us free from the power of sin.

Kraus admits this latter point, but then strangely argues that "justified by his blood" in Rom. 5:9-10 refers not to atonement but to the exaltation of Christ (on the basis of v. 11, cf. p. 183, n. 6). However, the thrust of vv. 9, 10 is not upon exaltation but upon "salvation from God's wrath" (v. 9). Along with Rom. 3:25 the forensic side of reconciliation is clearly intended. I can certainly agree with Kraus in his assertion that salvation involves "participation" in Christ and an acquiescence to his lordship. However, I do not understand the disjunctive thinking behind such statements as, "Certainly, to say that Jesus accepted responsibility for our guilt does not mean that he declared us acquitted of quilt. We are guilty, and we must confess our guilt" (p. 226). While it is true that guilt is "ontological, not merely legal" (p. 224), that does not mean the legal metaphor has thereby been obviated. While I appreciate the overall balance in the essay at this point, especially the attempt to redirect the balance with respect to those who make the forensic aspect the only model for atonement, I am disappointed at the downplaying of the legal side of atonement, especially since I agree with the Reformation perspective which makes the legal metaphor the basis of the others.

The second controversial issue is that of "deliverance from alien authorities" (pp. 182-86). Once again the problem is more in what is omitted than in what is stated. Kraus continues the metaphor of redemption from slavery in describing the victory over sin and Satan. However, he neglects the warfare metaphor of cosmic conflict, e.g. in the picture of sin establishing a "bridgehead" in us (Rom. 7:11, 23) or in the "armor of God" imagery (Eph. 6:10-18). In the same way that Yahweh is described as the "warrior of Israel" in the Old Testament, Christ is often seen as the divine "warrior" in the New Testament.[8] Moreover, Col. 2:15 speaks of Jesus "disarming the powers and authorities" and forcing them to participate in a "public spectacle" or victory procession. All in all the major metaphor is that of spiritual warfare. Furthermore, the linkage of "powers and authorities" with political, economic and social institutions (p. 186), while popular, is vigorously debated, and the arguments of those who disagree[9] should be discussed at least in a footnote.

The final major section ("Participating in Jesus' Salvation 'For us,'" chapters 12-14) is perhaps Professor Kraus's best example of contextualization, applying the concepts of the cross and reconciliation to modern issues. An excellent example is the section on "A Socio-Psychological View of Shame" (pp. 208f.), which shows how the biblical concept of shame fills a major gap in current psychological thinking regarding alienation, both from God and from others. However, again there is a lack of balance in the overall picture. While Kraus recognizes the presence of objective as well as subjective aspects to shame and guilt (p. 207), I wonder how complete his definition of the two sides might be. For Kraus subjective shame refers to feelings of failure and unworthiness while objective shame is social disgrace and exclusion. While these are adequate, they neglect the ontological aspect, namely the concept of imputed sin and guilt (Rom. 5:12f.). In the extended imagery of Adam's effect upon mankind (Rom 5:12f.), Paul distinctly connects Adam's sin with human sinfulness. While we certainly participate in this sinfulness (v. 12), there is nevertheless an inherited aspect to shame and guilt, and this should not remain undiscussed. Moreover, the three aspects (subjective, objective, ontological[10]) are not mutually exclusive but they coexist in Scripture.

I do not agree with Kraus, who follows Stendhal, that "a guilty conscience was Luther's problem, not St. Paul" (p. 214). Of the thirty occurrences of *syneidesis* in the New Testament, most are found in Paul, and Acts 24:16 (quoting Paul) states that Paul expends great effort to maintain a "clear conscience before God and man." In the pastorals the consciences of the false teachers are "corrupt" and "seared" (Tit. 1:15, 1 Tim. 4:2) and it is obvious that for Paul the conscience can only avoid guilt by maintaining a right relationship to God. In general "*syneidesis*" was an everyday Greek word which...had the morally bad negative sense of the pain that we feel when we do something wrong."[11] It has both negative connotations, referring to the shame or pain felt when doing wrong, and a positive connotation, referring to the power of moral discernment for making decisions. Therefore the conscience is indeed linked with guilt and its assuagement via the cross.

The discussion of Jesus' "vicarious identification" with our shame (ch. 13) is a further example of the tendency towards disjunctive thinking. Again it is a brilliant example of contextualization, linking the cross to the eastern concept of shame and demonstrating how Jesus has removed the alienation between humans and God and between one another by bearing the cross as an act of shame. This is a very real contribution to christological theory. However, it is unnecessary to thereby relegate the legal side of the equation to a secondary and relatively unimportant role. The two aspects, the legal and the moral, are interdependent. Sin as "debt" is essential to the biblical concept, as the Lord's Prayer demonstrates (Matt. 6:12, "forgive us our debts"). Yet at the same time sin as "transgression" of God's Law is equally intrinsic to the biblical picture (e.g. Rom. 4:7, 15).

In this light the definition of Jesus "despising the shame" in Heb. 12:2 as exposing "the despicable character of our humanly devised shame" (p. 222) cannot be upheld in the text. It is not our shame which is in view in Hebrews 12:2 but Jesus'; the phrase is certainly a reference back to Gethsemane when Jesus overcame the temptation to avoid the "shame" of the cross. How can Kraus in one section grant the legal aspect at least a secondary role (p. 224) and then on the next page reject it entirely ("The cross involved no equivalent compensation or payment of penalty demanded by God's anger," p. 225)? While it is true that "wrath" in the New Testament primarily refers to the final "wrath" to be experienced at the Last Judgment, the New Testament does not teach the dichotomy made above. In Rom. 5:9 the "justification" resulting from the cross "saves" us from present as well as the final "wrath" (cf. 1:18, 2:5). If one were to substitute "justice" for "anger" in the quote from page 225, the statement would fit closely the connection between "justification" as a legal concept and divine justice as taught in Romans 2:24-26. In short I can agree with everything said in this important chapter except for the unfortunate tendency to set the ethical side of the cross over against the judicial side. You cannot have one without the other!

It is in the final chapter on appropriating this salvation that the concept of *koinonia* or participation in Christ is most helpful. There is very little in this chapter with which one can take issue. I would want to stress that repentance is a turning from sin and a turning to Christ as well as adopting the mind of Christ; solidarity with Christ involves both aspects, which we might identify with the classical categories of conversion and sanctification. Yet at the same time there is no real distinction between the two. Conversion is the first moment of sanctification, and both entail a solidarity with Christ.

In conclusion, I applaud the monumental achievement of C. Norman Kraus in his contribution to Christology. It was a privilege to read it and an even greater privilege to participate in this consultation. The few observations or changes which I would encourage do not detract from his accomplishment. This is must reading for anyone who wishes to study in depth the christological teaching of Scripture.

Endnotes

1. On p. 19 of the preface Kraus recognizes the difficulty of obtaining literature in his changing situations in Japan and the United States. Therefore this is an observation rather than a criticism. Nevertheless it would have been helpful if he could have had access to such works as O'Collins (1983), Jewett, ed. (1984), or Fuller and Perkins (1983).

2. For a survey of these schools see my "Christology and New Testament Hermeneutics: A Survey of the Discussion" in Jewett (1984), 49-62.

3. Sobrino (1978); and Belo (1981).

4. Meyer (1979) and Gruenler (1982).

5. For an interesting use of this argument, see Fuller's use of this (in Jewett, ed., 1984, pp. 115-116) to establish the validity of an incarnational theology on the grounds that it coheres with Jesus' unique God-consciousness and filial awareness.

6. Note the interesting amalgamation of the cosmic conflict and redemptive sides of the equation under the rubric of "liberation" in Root, "Dying He Lives: Biblical Image, Biblical Narrative, and the Redemptive Jesus" in Jewett, ed. (1984), 154-69.

7. For a good summary see Packer (1974), 3-45; and Lyall (1984), 153-75.

8. See Longman (1982), 290-307.

9. See for instance O'Brien (1984), 110-50, for an excellent survey of the options and a strong defense of the view that "principalities and powers" are demonic rather than human institutions.

10. Kraus uses the term "ontological" of guilt but does so in contrast to the legal aspect, defining guilt thereby as "indebtedness and blameworthiness" (p. 224). Yet the ontology also includes the idea of imputation. While I agree with Cranfield that imputation must be defined as mediate rather than federal headship, i.e., we participate in the results of the sin inherited from Adam (v. 12), there is nevertheless a very real sense of legal imputation.

11. Colin Brown, "Conscience," *The New International Dictionary of New Testament Theology*, I, 351-52, following C. A. Pierce, *Conscience in the New Testament* (1955).

Bibliography

Belo, Fernando

1981 *A Materialist Reading of the Gospel of Mark*, tr. M. J. O'Connell. Maryknoll, N.Y.: Orbis Books.

Dunn, James D. G.

1980 *Christology in the Making: A New Testament inquiry into the Origins of the Doctrine of the Incarnation.* Philadelphia: Westminster Press.

Fuller, Reginald H. and Pheme Perkins

1983 *Who is This Christ? Gospel and Contemporary Faith.* Philadelphia: Fortress Press.

Gruenler, Royce

1982 *New Approaches to Jesus and the Gospels.* Grand Rapids: Baker Book House.

Jewett, Robert, ed.

1984 "Christology and Exegesis: New Approaches," *Semeia* 30.

Longman, Tremper, III

1982 "The Divine Warrior: The New Testament Use of an Old Testament Motif," *Westminster Theological Journal* 44, 290-307.

Lyall, Francis

1984 *Slaves, Citizens, Sons: Legal Metaphors in the Epistles*, Grand Rapids: Akademie Books.

Meyer, Ben

1979 *The Aims of Jesus.* London: SCM Press.

O'Brien, Peter T.

1984 "Principalities and Powers: Opponents of the Church," in D.
      A. Carson, ed., *Biblical Interpretation and the Church: The
      Problem of Contextualization.* Nashville: Thomas Nelson Pub-
      lishers.

O'Collins, Gerald

1983 *What Are They Saying About Jesus?"* second edition. New
      York: Paulist Press.

Packer, J. I.

1974 "What Did the Cross Achieve? The Logic of Penal Substitu-
      tion," *Tyndale Bulletin* 25, 3-45.

Sobrino, Jon.

1978 *Christology at the Crossroads: A Latin American Approach.*
      Maryknoll, N. Y.: Orbis Books.

CHAPTER 4
JESUS CHRIST OUR LORD FROM A MISSIOLOGICAL PERSPECTIVE

Fumitaka Matsuoka

My intent in this presentation is to review Dr. Kraus's book *Jesus Christ Our Lord: Christology from a Disciple's Perspective* in light of the emerging "ecumenical theology of pluralism." I hope this is a fitting contribution to Kraus's work particularly because this volume was shaped in part within the missiological context of Japan where he spent some time and also because of his claim that "Anabaptist theology ought to be a missionary theology."[1] Missiologically, furthermore, Kraus's work provides critical reflection upon the presuppositions and assumptions of Christologies that originate in the North Atlantic context.

In the past, religions as well as cultures have lived largely in isolation from one another. What is emerging today is a dialogical existence of religions and cultures out of their once separate and isolated places. The forces of modernity are compelling us to live together in the world rather than separately and competitively. It is the awareness of this compulsion that raises religious, cultural and ideological pluralism perhaps as a primary challenge to Christian faith.

A temptation is to either build spiritual ghettos in which people may live in isolation from one another or to follow the path of aggression with a view to dominating others. But both are destructive and possibly self-defeating options. A healthy alternative is to create a way, in the modern context of pluralism, for each religion, culture and worldview to relate with each other as community without losing its own ultimate spiritual basis.

An impending task for us Christians is to understand and interpret this pluralistic state of religions and cultures we encounter globally and locally from the standpoint of our ultimate commitment to Jesus Christ as the revelation of God. This ultimate commitment of ours is of course accompanied by many penultimate commitments, and finds expression in them. This is as true for Christians as for others. The search for human community is one such legitimate, penultimate expression of the ultimate commitment. A discussion on Christology needs necessarily to take this challenge seriously. The Anabaptist vision of salvation in Christ as renewal and restoration of humanity is a powerful metaphor in this respect.[2] What then is the theological basis of the search for this community of all humanity? What is the relation of the church, the community which acknowledges God as revealed in Jesus Christ, to the human community? Kraus's work on Christology speaks to these pertinent questions facing Christian faith and church today.

Christology--its present state

More has been written about Jesus in the last twenty years than in the previous two thousand years. The reason lies in part due to the increasingly pluralistic world of today that seeks to confess Christ in a variety of diverse settings. The present era is like that of the first century when the message of Jesus was refashioned by Paul and others into a thought-language that the larger gentile world, unfamiliar with Palestinian Judaism, could understand and accept. The reorientation of the gospel is the only possible way, in a new period, to believe in the same Christian faith. In every age we must try to embed the faith in a new setting, may it be culture, religion or worldview. This is the delicate function of hermeneutics because each new setting calls for Christians to respond to its own questions which may or may not be the familiar questions encountered in the past.

Professor Hideo Ohki of Tokyo Union Theological Seminary represents those who pose such a question in today's world. In his presentation several years ago entitled "Mission in Northeast Asia," Professor Ohki reviewed the history of Christianity from an "ecological point of view." According to Ohki's observation, the history can be viewed in three major segments. The first is the "pan Mediterranean era" (Corpus Christianum) when Christianity, which originated in Palestine, began to spread throughout over the Mediterranean world. It is the era when Christianity met the challenges of ancient Graeco-Roman religions, philosophies, and political powers and when ecclesiastical systems and doctrines were formulated. The second is the "pan Atlantic era" when Christianity expanded into the Americas from Europe and various denominations were established. As an antithesis to the European state-church system, the separation of church and state, civil liberty and rights became the cherished values during this period. The "pan-Pacific era" is the third in the development of the history of Christianity, according to Professor Ohki. This is an era when the Anglo-American Protestant Christianity is faced with the challenges of Northeast Asian cultures and religions, including Marxism.

The challenges facing Christianity in this "pan-Pacific era" are far more radical than those of the previous two eras, argues Ohki. The primary question posed in the "pan-Mediterranean era" was "What is Christianity?" It was doctrinal in nature, which called for an articulation of the nature of Christianity. The question of the "pan-Atlantic era" was "How is Christianity lived?" This question focused on the ethical and practical dimension of Christian faith. But today in the "pan-Pacific era" the primary question is "Why Christianity?" The raison d'etre of Christianity is being challenged in this era. This is the radical nature of the question.[3]

Christian response to this question, "Why Christianity?" does not come easily because it calls for self-examination of our long-held posture toward those who hold different perspectives toward life. It most likely calls for an abandonment of the belief in the supremacy of Christian faith in its relationship with other religions and worldviews. It also compels us to a much larger view of God, that is, what it really means to believe that there is one living God. In essence, this radical question posed to Christians today solicits from us nothing less than a *metanoia*.

In order to respond to the question "Why Christianity?" our Christian claim that Christ is indeed the Way, the Truth and the Life must be based on a response to the one living God of *all* the universes that may *ever* be discovered. If we begin from such a premise and take what Paul says in Romans about God never being without a witness, then we need to look with prophetic eye at all the history, culture and religion of people wherever they may. We need to recognize what God is doing wherever people exist in this world and be open to recognize the signs of God's presence and activity in the whole human history and culture, witnessing to the Way, the Truth and the Life wherever one finds it.

A fundamental theological stance needs to be developed in the recognition of the one living God incarnate in the life of all people. How can we proceed to do this task? What the North Atlantic Christians did as they began to build their own tradition from before Nicea and since, Christians in the places outside of the North Atlantic context need to do as well.

Missiologically, this means that we must go beyond indigenization, enculturation and contextualization. These approaches to the gospel merely suggest that what was being done in non-Western settings is different from what is being done in Western settings. This is an erroneous reading because in all settings one is faced with the historical reality on the one hand and the divine reality within that history on the other.

One does not start from a given body of Christianity such as the Western understanding of Christianity which resulted from a modification of biblical heritage mixed with Graeco-Roman culture and later on northern European culture. Even though one has to reckon with the mission history of a given setting, the starting point is a fundamental Christian belief in one God who has made and who continues to make Godself known to us through Jesus Christ.

This is to be recognized in every part of the life of people, for example, in the present social struggle for peace and justice in the Philippines or in the Korean community of Japan as much as in the major religious and cultural traditions. This does not mean to imply that all needs to be viewed as Christian but rather it confesses that God, whom we Christians seek to serve, is present in all human life and activities.

Methodologically, this moves us to a different starting point for theology. We no longer need to go on a large detour through European church history before we begin anything in another setting. We don't have to go through all the ramifications of European biblical scholarship, however much we might value it at certain points and use it selectively. The Bible still has a normative role, nevertheless. But the normativeness of the Bible is based on the faith conviction that what God did with the people of Israel, God has done or is doing or seeks to do with every people the world over. That makes the Bible normative.

On a more fundamental level, the only reason we would try to find God in the Bible is in order to find God everywhere. There is a need to suggest a theology which is living and dynamic but also a theology which is lived. We need to come back to recognizing the nature of Christian faith and theology which always must be a response to the living God where we are, in a very concrete historical reality.

Many past theological approaches are inadequately biblical because they don't recognize the extent to which the biblical record is always very particular, personal and concrete. The growth of modern Christologies has been plagued by a persistent reductionism. Some Christologies have attempted to take the riches of the gospel into the world. Biblical and ecclesiastical confession of Christian faith met the challenges of philosophies--from rationalism to idealism, neo-Kantianism, process thought, existentialism, and linguistic analysis. Others have evolved by reflection on Scripture and in obedience to the creedal traditions of the church.

There are two major traditions that set the tone of the development of Christologies in the North Atlantic setting. These traditions did so by holding in tension modernizing principle and material norm. Bultmann, on the one hand, treats Christology from an existentialist interpretation of the mythological character of the biblical message. The other tradition comes from the religionless interpretation of faith originated in Barth and Bonhoeffer. It begins with critical reflection on the biblical witness to Christ in light of its religionless character.

The dominance of these two strands in the development of modern Christologies ended with the "death of God" Christologies which became basically soteriology. Contemporary developments are characterized by the search of new starting points and different categories instead of the refinement of existing alternatives.[4] In Altizer and Hamilton the tension between critical principle and material norm that characterizes the development of modern Christology has ceased. The modern critical principle became the material norm and has taken down the confines of Christological formulations. It has transformed Christology into a principle of cultural interpretation.

Powerful responses to the dissolution of the boundary of modern Christology has taken the expression of (1) the future-oriented Christologies of Dorothee Sölle (Christ as the "Representative"), Jürgen Moltmann, Wolfhart Pannenberg, Schubert Ogden, John Cobb and others. Rather than believing God's absence is because of God's non-existence, the future-oriented Christologies believe God's absence is the result of God's not-yet-being; (2) of the Word-Event (Gerhard Ebeling, Ernst Fuchs) which claim that God is "hidden" from people because of the crisis in language. The new hermeneutics has thus become an attempt to renew human language so it can become the means of knowing God.

The development of modern Christology is grounded in the culture of Western people. Both the rejection and the acceptance of modern thought in Christology still retained the cultural basis of theology which is Western civilization. Even though theologians are aware that Christology reflects cultural involvements, there has been little reason to put this insight to a test. However, this situation has been changing. The social, political, economic revolution of marginalized peoples, both within the West and in other parts of the world, is precipitating a religious revolution as well. What is called for is a reorientation in theology so that it utilizes, recognizes, and reclaims resources of people wherever they are. This is a call to reclaim one's own heritage as Asian or African and the marks of God's presence in ones own history, society and culture. What is being abandoned is the erroneous notion that the more Western one is, the more Christian one becomes. Furthermore, what is common to the Christologies of marginalized people, both in the West and in the rest of the world, is that redemption is viewed as involving the transformation of the social, political and economic powers that create the conditions of consciousness.

> I think what we have today is an explosion of pluralities. All efforts to reduce to unity are over. This is not without precedent. In the first century A.D. Christianity was not a unity, it was a plurality of different approaches.... Perhaps what we're seeing as the Church enters its third millennium is a reprise.[5]

Contribution of Kraus's Christology

The "explosion of pluralities" of which Sheehan speaks presents significant challenges to formulations of the Christian faith. As feminists in the U.S. and the deconstructionists in France have pointed out, the price of shaping traditions is that traditions are formed in acts of violence that demand the repression of certain themes, and those submerged themes will continue to stalk the tradition. Repressed themes are indeed reemerging and finding their voice in our time as Christianity struggles to reconceptualize itself as a truly inclusive, worldwide phenomenon.

But such a task of reconceptualization carries with it various concerns for Christology. One has to do with methodological problems. Can rules be formulated to aid in the movement of meaning across cultural and other boundaries of difference? Obviously, people from different environments can and do communicate, but what makes that possible and what impedes communication is still only imperfectly understood. As Kraus accurately points out, "Each culture has its worldview--its concept of being (ontology) and modes of analogy."[6] What is the mode of analogy that is appropriate to communicate the event of Christ in today's world?

The second area of concern is a theological one. In our embrace of genuine pluralism, what happens to the unity and normativity of Christian faith? There is one kind of attitude, masked as pluralism, that is sometimes really a form of indifference or even of solipsism, in that it refuses to evaluate any of the proposed positions. It becomes an excuse to abandon the struggle for truth and gets used as a hedge against an outside challenge.

A third area of concern is the purpose of Christological endeavors in the increasingly pluralistic world of today. This is the "Why Christianity" question. This question challenges Christians more than ever before to articulate their faith in such a way as to clarify the meaning of Christ being truly the Way, the Truth, and the Life.

Today any attempt for Christological formulation needs to recognize the reality that there is no longer sufficient environmental commonality. Any message, which certainly includes the Good News, is not necessarily communicated from the sender to receiver in the way it was originally intended. Quite likely, the receiver of the message situates it differently within the receiver's own universe than the sender would have done or, because of the strangeness of the message, isolates it from other knowledge as an alien message. Thus the communication environment of sender and receiver is not necessarily coterminous. In today's world we need to begin with the assumption that difference is indeed a central category. What is needed is a discipline on the part of the message-giver for a more dialogical approach to allow the receiver of the message to open up to the sender both personal and cultural experience, and then allowing a continuing conversation that helps the receiver situate the message into his or her universe.

This involves recognizing the difference of the other and allowing time for each party to explore the universe of the partner in order to promote more effective communication thereafter. Learning to listen on the part of the message-giver is an essential task for effective communication.

Theological language is indeed the language of analogy. It is highly significant to recognize that "historical experience can function *only as a metaphor* of the divine self-giving."[7] Communication takes place when we can in fact acknowledge that "In religious language we speak of this [the reality of God] as a *sacramental* presence which is at once real on the historical level and yet points to a metahistorical reality beyond itself."[8] Such confessional courage makes the communication for Christians possible in today's world.

Kraus speaks of "contextualizing the language of self-disclosure" of God in Christ Jesus. It is precisely in what he terms as "(1) the nature of human personhood and personal relationships and (2) the nature of our religious experience as a social relationship of God with people" that such a self-revelation of God takes place.[9] This statement has a two-fold significance: (1) Effective communication, particularly across cultural and social distance, must learn how to negotiate that boundary of otherness. The only way to accept the other as other is to admit the possibility of change on the part of the self. Obviously the acceptance of otherness is very hard and painful to attain, not only because of the actual differences to be accepted, but also because the other summons up within persons and within cultures issues that have been repressed. (2) The statement also means that any communication needs to be dialogical in approach. Not only is reciprocity in communication important, but more significantly, questions may be asked as modes of challenge, and not just for information. This is a delicate but necessary dimension of interpreting meaning across boundaries of culture and difference. Not to challenge may be construed as not taking the new formulation seriously or as being indifferent to difference. Modes of respect and trust are essential. A dialogue is a dialogue of commitment.

"Why did Jesus have to die?" Kraus's Christology grew out of an attempt to respond to this question. This is a question of normativity and the tradition of Christian faith. It has become increasingly clear in recent years that linguistic criteria alone cannot of itself provide for the resolution of what constitutes confessions of truth. Already at the time of the Monophysite controversy language broke down as an adequate criterion for confession. The number of language families now involved in Christianity makes confession of truth even more of a problem. Formulae, in themselves, can provide necessary but not sufficient conditions for establishing normativity.

This means that a different criteriology must be established. It seems that only a battery of multiple criteria is an adequate approach. A univocal criterion such as "if it does not liberate, it is not Christian" is true, but cannot capture the entire reality at stake. Univocal criteria depend upon a great deal of ambiguity to function, and this ambiguity has regularly opened the way to ideological distortion. One need only *think* how a *sola scriptura* criterion has been invoked through the centuries.

Understanding what those multiple criteria should be is an important task toward creating a Christology in today's diverse and pluralistic world. Kraus's participatory approach to the meaning of the event of Christ, "solidarity with Christ," opens up otherwise parochial and often dogmatic approaches to the normativity of Christian faith. It invites an openness toward radically new possibilities. Solidarity and *koinonia* with Christ invokes in the Christian a willingness to be shaped in the new life in the midst of the old, a radically unexpected way of life, the paradigm of which is the cross of Christ. That this perception of Christ is grounded in a particular contingent place of history, i.e., the Anabaptist tradition, provides the credibility for Dr. Kraus's Christology.

Theologically we live today in a polycentric church. What is needed is the confidence of faith which allows for different configurations of ideas within each culture and different valences assigned to ideas therein while seeking to affirm the coherence of faith in each theology. Kraus's work helps us to move toward such a task.

Endnotes

1. C. Norman Kraus, *Jesus Christ Our Lord: Christology from a Disciple's Perspective* (Scottdale, Pa.: Herald Press, 1987), 15.

2. Or, as Kraus expresses this Anabaptist reading of salvation, "the ultimate goal of the new covenant ratified in Christ's cross is none other than the realization of the original covenant intention in an actual universal reconciled community under God (Eph. 2:14-16)," p. 178.

3. Hideo Ohki, "Mission in Northeast Asia--A Theological Discussion," *Keisei* (September 1983).

4. Bultmann's insistence on relating the possibility of authentic existence to "the particular historical (historisch) event of Jesus of Nazareth" met a powerful critique in Shubert M. Ogden. He argues that there is a structural inconsistency in Bultmann's thought. If authentic existence is possible "in principle" apart from Jesus, Ogden points out, then it is also separable "in fact." Thus there should be no limit to the application of demythologizing. This challenge opens up the possibility of a "Copernican revolution" in Christology in the thought of John Hick and others.

Barth's thought is characterized by his thorough-going Christocentrism and his rejection of natural theology. This structural frame of reference was radicalized in the thought of Bonhoeffer and subsequently by the "death of God" theologians. Paul M. van Buren, for example, pushes Barth's Christocentrism into an absolute Christomonism. Faith, he insists, does not point to the way Jesus Christ reveals God, but how he defines a new option for human existence.

5. Quoted in Thomas Sheehan, "Who Do Men Say That I Am?" *The Atlantic Monthly* (December 1986), 58.

6. Kraus, *Jesus Christ Our Lord*, p. 44.

7. Ibid., p. 56.

8. Ibid., p. 57.

9. Ibid., p. 120.

CHAPTER 5
PASTORAL ISSUES IN *JESUS CHRIST OUR LORD*

Melvin D. Schmidt

I grew up with what you might call a highly exalted view of the MAN. I was sure he never went to the bathroom. Of course, he never had a lustful thought, and was in fact totally without sexual feelings. By extension, I also figured out, at a very early age, that this MAN's representative, our pastor, also did not go to the bathroom, and his four children were immaculately conceived. After all, I reasoned, if it happened in the Bible with holy people, why should it not happen now with holy people? I was asking the right hermeneutical question, but my nascent docetism was getting in the way of getting the right answers.

Fortunately, I grew up and put away childish things. But I was well into adulthood before I totally lost my innocence on the question of the humanity of Jesus. In fact, I was pastor of a small town church in Kansas, having just finished seminary, and I was preaching my way through the book of Hebrews. I had a collision with the fifth chapter of Hebrews, where it seemed to me that Jesus was portrayed as having *earned* his status as son of God, rather than having been born with it. Could it be that Jesus *decided* to be the Messiah, God's chosen, and hence his only begotten Son? I asked myself. I had never thought of Jesus in that manner before. I had never confronted that possibility, yet it seemed to me that the book of Hebrews insists on such a view of Jesus. The sinlessness of this man, according to Hebrews, is not the result of divine infusion of some sort, making him a superman or supernatural person. His sinlessness lies rather in the realm of his obedience to the will of the Father, and it came as a result of conscious decision and moral struggle.

So I preached a sermon on "The humanity of Christ" sometime in 1968. Among other things, I said the following:

"The greatest and most astonishing apostasy which continually rears its head within the church is the denial of the humanity of

Jesus Christ. Such a denial is indeed a stab at the very heart of our faith. But somehow, in one way or another, this apostasy is constantly maintained by some believers who are convinced that Jesus was not really a human being. He had a divine nature of which you and I cannot partake."

Soon after that, I was asked by our denominational paper, *The Mennonite*, to write an article. Believe me, I was ready. I condensed and sent in my sermon on the humanity of Christ, and had a sentence which was to cause me no end of trouble. The sentence reads as follows:

"You have nothing to offer the world if you cannot offer a human Christ, a red blooded male who had bad breath and dandruff."

This statement caused a small flood of letters to the editor and to me personally. Some said it wasn't true: Jesus did not have bad breath and dandruff. Others said it was true but it shouldn't have been said. One letter which I received from a brother in Minneapolis took six pages, single-spaced, typewritten on both sides, to explain that he was greatly relieved to discover something he had suspected all along but had never allowed himself to think.

My personal journey with the MAN Jesus has been a life-long quest, and will continue to be so. This same journey has also been the journey of the church for two thousand years. The publication of C. Norman Kraus's *Jesus Christ Our Lord* is one more significant step in that long journey. It is a step which I believe brings us closer to maturity on the issue of Christology in the Mennonite church. We are "coming of age" regarding how we understand Jesus. The rest of this essay will seek to deal with how the process of maturation will and should impinge on the church. The writer of the book of Hebrews had no illusions about the difficulty of accepting a radically human view of the man Jesus. Following the passage which sets forth this radically human oriented view of the man who with "loud cries and tears" offered prayers to God for deliverance from his death, but who, nevertheless "learned obedience through what he suffered," we are given a rather tactless rebuke: such a view of Jesus is not for those who have become willfully "dull of hearing," (Heb. 5:11) but is rather for those who are ready for "solid food." It is not for those who are "unskilled in the word of righteousness," i.e., living on milk. Maturity in Christ calls us toward the solid food of his human life, a life that by definition has no advantages over the rest of humanity "physically, psychologically, morally, and spiritually" (Kraus, p. 67).

Here I would offer four points in response to Kraus's work:

1) Kraus notes in his preface that for three hundred years

theology has been done largely as a university discipline, and he rightfully proposes that it is time to move it into the ranks of the followers of Christ, i.e., the church. Hence, his subtitle, "Christology from a Disciple's Perspective." Kraus's efforts to begin the conversation from another point of view are to be lauded. It is fair to question whether he accomplishes what he sets out to do. The answer to this question, in my opinion, is in doubt. This book is not Christology from a disciple's perspective unless it is assumed that the disciple is a Ph.D. well versed in scholarly disciplines. The conversation that Kraus has begun probably had to begin with a book like this, written by a professional for professionals, but the conversation must now move outward and inward into the church. My concern can be stated as follows: Can Norman Kraus's book be effectively used as a study document by laypeople in the church? The answer is NO. It is not an easily discussed book but discussable materials should be written from it, and it will be a tragedy if our church leaders do not take up this conversation.

2) If the theological reformulation begun by Kraus is accepted as a serious task in the church, our educational task will be to guide and prod persons toward the mature christology which he sets forth. The educational implications of such a task are enormous and probably neverending, but our commitment to such educational goals should never be in question. Some of the educational implications of such a Christology are already known through the work of James Fowler and others who have formulated spiritual "growth stages." We do not expect a child to understand Jesus in the same way that an adult understands Jesus, but there should be clarity among us about what we teach our children and what we expect in terms of spiritual growth in adulthood. Too much of the time, I fear, we have been satisfied to let adults in the church retain a very childlike view of Jesus. We have not challenged the immature "superman" concepts which children typically have, and should be encouraged in. We have not challenged our adults to reformulate their thinking about the miracles of Jesus and the virgin birth along the lines suggested by C. Norman Kraus.

3) Kraus has given us an urgent agenda to work on in the church. While each person will ultimately decide how to respond to this agenda, it seems to me that a danger of spiritual elitism is created by the very fact that we have the agenda at all. My misgivings about this agenda are based on the experiences I have already had in a church in which a widening theological gap already exists between congregation and college, congregation and seminary, and ultimately, pulpit and pew. The pastoral issue here is that a commitment must be made at all levels, including individual pastors, to nar-

rowing the gap instead of widening it. As a pastor, if I take Kraus's book seriously and end up with a Christology quite different from that of the conventional Protestantism it is incumbent upon me as a pastor to share with my congregation whatever views I have on Christology. I would be a charlatan if I were to do otherwise.

4) As our thinking about the man Jesus Christ evolves, I believe that narrative theology will become a helpful tool for the church. A significant beginning has been made in our church and other denominations toward understanding the biblical stories as stories rather than statements of systematic theology. We are learning how to extrapolate less theory from the stories of scripture even as we are learning to enjoy them more.

The goal of narrative theology has not been reached, however, until persons begin to share *their own* stories. Indeed, the biblical stories themselves have no more value than novelty if they stay in the realm of story and never enter the realm of personal experience. Adam's story is my story. I have done precisely what Eve did. The story of Israel is our story as well as his-story.

Thus, my sharing of the Jesus story implies not only that I share *his* story but also that I share *my* story in relationship to his story. I began this essay with my story, not because I believe that my story is normative for anyone else, nor because I consider my story to be more important than anyone else's. I began with my story because I consider it important to share our history with regard to Jesus quite self-consciously. Then we can understand why Jesus means one thing to one person and another thing to another person.

C. Norman Kraus has performed an invaluable service to the church in terms of establishing the framework within which we share the Jesus story and our stories. His work challenges us to grow toward maturity in christological understandings. This growth toward maturity is a process which the biblical story itself mandates.

CHAPTER 6
JESUS CHRIST OUR LORD IN HISTORICAL ANABAPTIST PERSPECTIVE

Cornelius J. Dyck

We have in this volume a unique attempt to do theology in a non-traditional way. The language, categories, objectives and methodology are delightfully different from the discourse of 1500 years to which we have become accustomed. This makes for interesting and provocative reading. The number of biblical references are impressive and seem to be exegetically foundational rather than only supportive of meanings arrived at on other grounds, even though the author's approach is more theological than exegetical. The cross-cultural references are substantive and refreshing. The book is obviously the fruit of many years of study, dialogue and reflection. In any case, I find it refreshing and helpful in understanding the nature and mission of Christ.

With all of these variables in approach, however, we are entitled to ask whether the essential aspects of the subject have been covered, whether the treatment is complete or whether there are major omissions. Similarly we ask whether there are extraneous materials which unduly encumber the account. Are there evident biases which hinder the asking of vital questions or lead a-priori to predictable conclusions? Which traditions are being discarded and with what results? Can the new language used carry the necessary freight of meaning? These are actually questions of methodology. The focus of the following comments then will be primarily in the areas of method and of doctrine.

The function of tradition

The concept of primitivism entered Believers Church historiography nearly a century ago implicitly in the writings of Ludwig Keller and others, but it became a major category for understanding sixteenth-century Anabaptism first in Franklin H. Littell's 1958 volume on *The Anabaptist View Of The Church*. "The dominant theme in the thinking of the main-line Anabaptists was the recovery of the life and virtue of the Early Church" (79). "The Church of the Restitution" was his preferred term. By this he believed the Anabaptists meant a return to the message and example of the New Testament as a binding norm to be followed by the true church. In this they differed from the major Reformers who adapted select early church motifs to their own time. While the intention of the Reformers also was the recovery of the gospel message, they could not break with the heritage of the past on Constantinianism, that is church and state intimacy, elements of the sacramental system, including baptism, and other issues.

In *Jesus Christ Our Lord* Kraus uses a methodology that is more rigorously primitivist even than Littell's early work. It goes further in relativizing the history of the post-apostolic church than most Anabaptists did. It is an attempt to take the Bible seriously as the primary and only major source for Christology.

This does not, of course, resolve the question of hermeneutics applied or appropriated. The classical Greek metaphysical definitions of Nicea are avoided, except for occasional cross-references in the notes--no homoousious/homoiousious (same substance/like substance), no "begotten, not made" (all of which the three Cappadocians were to make into a God with three personalities and an impersonal essence), and no definitions of Chalcedon--no Theotokos/Christotokos (Mother of God/Mother of Christ), no "truly God and truly man." In place of these concepts the historical Jesus is described "from below" (Ritschl), that is, as a truly historical person, based on the *Gestalt* which emerges from the Gospels. Metaphor is a crucial historical and personal analogy for the author: "Jesus himself is the metaphor of God. He is the 'Word of God' and the 'Event' of salvation in which God is present to us in our historical existence" (57).

Who would not agree that the highly politicized and divisive creeds of the fourth and fifth centuries have created both havoc and confusion in the church in centuries past, and that a fresh contemporary formulation could become a real asset? Nevertheless, these creeds are a very important part of the history of the church, our history, which those who read only the present volume would not get to know without more traditional historical studies. We might respond by saying that Believers Church people do not use creeds anyway. True, but this becomes all the more reason for knowing this history, particularly in the absence of liturgy and other bridges to the past in this tradition.

The councils which formulated these creeds were significant stages in the development of doctrine and, sometimes wrongly, in identifying heresy. There were also many centuries of significant church historical-theological developments since then, many giants of the faith, martyrs and simple believers. To go from the New Testament to the rationalism of the nineteenth century, with brief attention to the Greek fathers, a nod to Anselm and Abelard and occasional dialogue in the sixteenth century and on to the present undercuts both historical and theological understanding. Without in the least denying the authority of Scripture, does it not seem just a trifle presumptuous to largely ignore nearly 2000 years of Christian experience in the formulation of doctrine? Given the present church inclination to do just that we do not need further encouragements to pole-vault from the New Testament to the present with relative indifference to the "in-between."

Most Anabaptist writers would have agreed with Menno who accepted the four Ecumenical Councils of Nicea (325), Constantinople (381), Ephesus (431) and Chalcedon (451), but placed them under the authority of Scripture (CWMS, pp. 525, 703, 754, 761, etc.).[1] They had limited authority.

But this is not a volume on church history. We note that the author places the work of Christ into the total context of our Lord's incarnation, life, death and resurrection. Jesus' death was not predestined but chosen freely by him on our behalf. It was the inevitable result of how he lived, what he did and who he was that drove his opponents to crucify him (Rom. 5:10). In our present culture Passion Week church services have tended to accent primarily Jesus' suffering and death, by which we can be saved, without including the "saved by his life" motif as an integral part of his total work ending in the cross and resurrection. In thus emphasizing Jesus' earthly ministry, including a strong emphasis on his humanity, the historical is indeed affirmed. So also the author's repeated rejection of docetism affirms the historical. In Anabaptism Marpeck stands out as the most vital defender of the humanity of Christ--against the spiritualizing Schwenckfeld. Still, I have an uneasy feeling of loss here, that more than bath water has been poured out in so lightly treating the long struggle of the church to be faithful in a very crucial area of faith.

The nature of Christ

Nowhere am I struck more with the inadequacy of human language than in chapter five where Kraus struggles with the preexistence of Jesus and the nature of the identity of the Godhead.

In order to preserve our sanity (and orthodoxy) one is tempted to say "let us simply decide to call it a mystery," as the Anabaptists did in Strasbourg in 1555 and later when they urged each other not to know more (about the incarnation) than the Scriptures teach. It is possible to want to know more than is given for us to know, which has been called original sin since Adam and Eve tried it.

How shall we talk about preexistence, incarnation, trinity, the unity and individuality of the Godhead without using Greek essence terms or repeating the old heresies of subordinationism or modalism or adoptionism or denying the deity of Jesus as the Christ? It seems to me that Kraus has cited most of the relevant texts and presented most of the cogent arguments, including the implications these issues have for our understanding of creation and for ethics. Still, the proposal that the solution may lie in adopting "an analogy of personal identity and sense of selfhood" (p. 114, cf. p. 120) calls for more testing though this relational image may be more appealing than the ontological. Psychological categories may be "in" today, but not necessarily more helpful than to speak of "essential unity...an identity of essence" as Pannenberg does (112) in the classical mode. How can the simple yet profound Logos Christology of John 1:1-5 be made more functional theologically? Lay people seem to have less problem with this text than intellectuals! (Matt. 11:27).

In discussing the humanity of Jesus the author includes an excursus on the virgin birth (pp. 74-79), which he affirms as miracle and as a witness "to the true origin and identity of Jesus as the Christ of God...." He rightly affirms that the New Testament does not make this a proof of the deity of Christ. Deity is more easily based, I would think, on his life and work and on statements like "He who has seen me has seen the Father" (John 14:9), "I and the Father are one" (John 10:30), and other dominical identity texts. The linking of virgin birth with deity has, unfortunately, been made a test of true faith in all kinds of orthodoxies ever since Augustine denigrated the human body in defining original sin.

The answer of the medieval church to the necessity of a sinless Jesus was the dogma of the immaculate conception. Menno Simons' response was to stress the heavenly flesh Christology of Hoffman and others.[2] Menno, Dirk Philips and the Melchiorites were definitely not docetic, which the author recognizes (p. 65, n. 1), but often sounded as though they were (p. 49, n. 6). A fully human Jesus, including human freedom of the will, is necessary for discipleship, even as a fully divine Christ is necessary for salvation. We can indeed say "he was vulnerable to making mistakes" (p. 70) but the classical belief of the church has been that Jesus could sin but did not (John 8:46). Does vulnerable imply more than that? Is it helpful in affirming his humanity to say that he was "conceived out of wedlock" (p. 218)? Was he? Betrothal did not permit co-habitation; it was more than simply an engagement since divorce was required to dissolve it. It may be that these are no more than illustrations of the volatility of the new language mode, but again, it "feels" as though more is implied. All Anabaptists believed in the sinlessness of Christ. The Polish Brethren were not Anabaptists.

Belief in the incarnation as miraculous was central to the Anabaptist view of salvation. It is necessary not to support the deity of Jesus, though it does do that, but because it is the beginning of the total sequence of salvation events through to the resurrection. It is also not a test of the extent to which we affirm biblical authority because the texts in Matthew (1:18) and Luke (1:26ff.) are clear enough. It is more a question of what we do with these texts. Biblical silence on the virgin birth, especially Paul's, does not negate these texts. One of the repeated arguments of the Anabaptists was: where the Scriptures speak, we speak; where they are silent, we are silent (Hubmaier). Here the Scriptures do speak.

The work of Jesus Christ

The cross as theodicy (chapter eight) seems to me to be a particularly helpful statement of the issues involved! Judgment on sin is not denied, but the love which found its ultimate expression on the cross holds the key. The cross is not only God's answer to evil, but also a paradigm for discipleship. Here the Believers Church parts company with Protestantism and all sacramentalism. Even some emphases in Christian experience which are close to our spiritual life and not to be despised -- the personal experience of the forgiveness of sin, inner peace and joy, an assurance of salvation, new faith, hope and love--need to be placed into the context of this understanding of the cross and atonement. Salvation goes beyond feeling to ethics and being.

Thus the author writes: "Salvation is not exclusively a *spiritual* phenomenon. That is, it is not simply a theologically defined change in the way God regards us. Neither is it merely a *future* possibility for which the present age of suffering provides a continuing time of preparation and testing. It is a real--though at present incomplete--change in the human condition including all its dimensions--spiritual, social, and physical" (p. 172). Amen!

Two issues should be identified here: deification (the image metaphor, p. 194 ff.) and the nature of grace. On page 196 Kraus states that "we should probably avoid the language of divinization." Perhaps holiness or sanctification would be more acceptable? In any case, most Anabaptists believed that conversion led to a new nature, an ontological change. Note the words of Dirk Philips: "All believers are partakers of the divine nature...yea, gods and children of the most high, in like manner as Christ on earth and in heaven, then they are still not of the identical essence and person that God and Christ are. Oh no, the creature never becomes the Creator, and that flesh and word never become the eternal spirit itself, which God is, for that is impossible."[3] Believers take on the likeness of Christ as they follow him (Rom. 8:29; 1 Cor. 5:17f.).

This is a clear rejection of forensic justification and a defining of the continuing power of the Holy Spirit in the life of the believer. The believer participates in the life in Christ and is transformed daily more nearly into his image. This is a particularly Johannine motif held by most Anabaptists, including Denck, but not by Hubmaier or Marpeck. Calvin's comment about the Anabaptist "illusion of perfection" (p. 195, n. 5) may sound unfair, but is just below the surface in many instances of the use of the ban. A few second generation Anabaptists did teach perfection.

What, we may then ask, is the nature of grace? Is it the transformation experienced by the believer as the divine image takes shape in him or her? And is this purely a gift or a synergistic achievement? For grace to be grace it must be by definition total. And this is indeed what we have in Anabaptism. Kraus correctly speaks of renewal "as a work of God in us" (p. 195). One of the significant contributions of J. A. Oosterbaan to Anabaptist studies is to show the close correlation between creation and atonement in Menno and others. "The Christ of creation is the same as the Christ of the atonement."[4] He who creates (John 1:1-5) is also the One who recreates to newness of life. It is because Christ is one, at creation and redemption, that Menno and most Anabaptists had trouble with the Chalcedonian (451) two natures Christology as they saw it in Roman Catholicism and the Protestant Reformers. It always seemed to slip into a greater emphasis upon his divinity than his humanity.

Was this tendency not also true of Menno's "heavenly flesh" Christology? No, because, according to Oosterbaan, "The Word did not *take on* flesh but himself *became* flesh. Jesus did not receive his body from Mary; He himself became a body which was received by Mary in faith...."[5] This is a more radical rejection of Mariology than we find in Luther or Calvin. Because Christ is one Menno's Christology begins at creation. Thus he writes:

> By grace the human race was created through Jesus Christ
>   when as yet it was not.
> By grace it was accepted through Christ when it was lost.

By grace Christ was sent to us of the Father. John 3:34.
By grace he has sought the lost sheep, taught repentance
and remission of sins, and died for us when we were
yet ungodly and enemies.
By grace it is given us to believe.
By grace the Holy Spirit was given us in the name of Jesus.
John 14:16.
In short, by grace eternal life is given us through Christ
Jesus.[6]

It is important here to underscore the latent implications of
Kraus because Anabaptism has so often been accused of lacking a
central doctrine of grace and thus of encouraging work-
righteousness. Grace is the love of God. Wherever this love is at
work it brings forth that which formerly was not. It creates and
recreates. This approach can provide a stronger base for
discipleship--being co-workers with God in and through Christ--than
Nachfolge or an *imitatio Christi* motif.[7]

The limitations of language are again apparent when we
speak of "a balance between faith and work" in Anabaptism, or place
faith and work in sequence where faith is "a living relationship and
works simply the product of regeneration" (p. 236). In Anabaptism
faith and works were seen as one. But we are rescued by phrases
like "solidarity or *koinonia* with Christ" and by the use of Paul's "in
Christ." Participation and identification are strong words in this context. Faith and works were, we might say, synonymous, indivisible,
bonded, mutually fulfilling. As James' epistle put it, faith was com-
pleted by works.... (James 2:22, 25; cf. Matt. 25:31ff.) and "was not
also Rahab the harlot justified by works?"

We need further clarification on one final point. All the
excellent statements in this last chapter notwithstanding, can we
really say that Christ's mission (vocation) was qualitatively no different than that of his disciples and our own? (p. 242). God truly has
many daughters and sons, but One is more than "first among equals"
(Cyprian); he was and is unique (*einmalig*, i.e., once for all). Yes, in
a way we are all called to be "little Christs" (Luther) to our neigh-
bors, but not in the way Paul speaks of Christ's mission in Romans
5:1: "...we have peace with God through our Lord Jesus Christ." We
cannot put our own names there. I do not fully understand the
intention of this phrase.

Christ and history

In the Christian context Christ has normally been taken to have

significant meaning for understanding history. He has been called
the beginning and end (Alpha and Omega) of history, the center of
history, the Lord of history, the true meaning of history, etc. In him
time divided into before and after, not only on the calendar of world
events, but also personally--a new order has already begun (2 Cor.
5:17). Life will never be the same since Jesus Christ came and,
ultimately, the believer looks to him for its meaning. I say this even
though, as an historian, I resonate more with the "one history"
approach represented today by Pannenberg than the two-history
approach of sacred (Heilsgeschichte) and secular (Weltgeschichte).
Christ is the most powerful Word ever spoken in history! Christology tells us that in the events of history, even the holocaust, the last
word has not yet been spoken. God is still at work until all things
become part of the kingdom of our Lord and of his Christ.

I miss (or missed) any references to this in the volume. I am
not talking about a chapter on eschatology as a "fitting conclusion" to
the book, but about Christology as a central motif to the interpretation of history and without which the entire discussion remains
incomplete at many points.

Endnotes

1. *The Complete Writings Of Menno Simons.* (Scottdale: Herald Press, 1956).

2. See S. Voolstra, *Het Woord Is Vlees Geworden* (Kampen: Uitgevermaatschappij J. H. Kok, 1982). Also William E. Keeney, *The Development Of Dutch Anabaptist Thought And Practice From* 1539-1564 (Nieuwkoop: B. de Graaf, 1968).

3. *Bibliotheca Reformatoria Neerlandica* X, 148-149.

4. J. A. Oosterbaan, "The Theology of Menno Simons," *Mennonite Quarterly Review*, Vol. XXXV, No. 3 (July 1961), 192.

5. Ibid.

6. *Opera Omnia Theologica* (1681), 463. From J. A. Oosterbaan, "Grace in Dutch Mennonite Theology," in *A Legacy Of Faith*, Cornelius J. Dyck, editor (Newton, Kansas: Faith and Life Press, 1962), 81.

7. See also Alvin J. Beachy, *The Concept Of Grace In The Radical Reformation* (Nieuwkoop: B. de Graaf, 1977).

CHAPTER 7
THEOLOGICAL REFLECTIONS ON *JESUS CHRIST OUR LORD*

I. John Hesselink

First, I would like to commend the presidents of the Associated Mennonite Biblical Seminaries for sponsoring this consultation on C. Norman Kraus's significant new book on Christology. It is a creative, thoughtful and provocative book and accordingly merits this kind of attention, quite apart from its historical significance within the Mennonite community.

This is the way to do theology, i.e., in dialogue and personal encounter. Thereby an important theological study receives the critical attention it deserves, and more important, the key issues in such a study can then be sharpened, tested, and refined. Rarely, however, is such an opportunity provided in this country, whereas in Europe this is not uncommon. For example, one of the highlights of my sabbatical in the Netherlands in the fall of 1985 was to attend an all-day consultation devoted to the very stimulating, provocative book by the young Leiden University theologian, A. van de Beek (Hendrikus Berkhof's successor), *Waarom? over lijden, schuld en God (Why? Concerning Suffering, Guilt, and God)*. Evaluations and critiques were given by a systematic theologian, an ethicist, and a university chaplain. This was followed by a response by the author and a discussion. The various papers and the response were later published in a book entitled *Nogmaals: Waarom?*

Such ventures are not only theologically stimulating and encouraging--and perhaps also chastening--for the author, but through such a process truth is served and the church is edified.

Secondly, I would like to express my appreciation for the privilege of being invited to contribute one of the responses and participate in this consultation as an "outsider," i.e., non-Mennonite. I take it I owe the invitation in part to my acquaintance with President Marlin Miller, which goes back to our first encounter in Basel, Switzerland in the summer of 1960. Our subsequent contacts in the 1970s were at meetings of the Association of Theological Schools. (I served as president of Western Seminary from 1973 until 1985). These contacts were few and brief, however, until my wife and I enjoyed a delightful Sunday dinner with the Millers earlier this spring.

A more important reason for my participation is the fact that we served as missionaries in Japan for many years (1953-1973). Thus it was felt that perhaps I could speak to the shame motif which is so powerful in Japanese culture and which plays an important role in the latter part of Kraus' book where he links shame and guilt and gives special prominence to the former.

Moreover, one of my colleagues at Tokyo Union Seminary, where I taught for twelve years (1961-1973), was Kazoh Kitamori, author of the famous book *Theology of the Pain of God*. This has also influenced Dr. Kraus' thinking (see p. 216).

Since the Krauses also served as missionaries in Japan for several years--although after our departure--we also have this in common. Thanks to some mutual missionary friends, we met each other earlier this year and were able to share some of our experiences in Japan. It was also possible for Dr. Kraus to participate in one of my theology classes.

I am especially grateful for this personal encounter in view of the fact that there is much in the book with which I disagree. Having come to know Norman Kraus as a gracious, winsome Christian gentleman helps mitigate some of the hostility I felt as my theological hero, John Calvin, and the Reformed tradition were being attacked from time to time. Disagreements can be dealt with in a much more Christian manner when a prior positive personal relationship has been established.

In addition, I was favorably disposed toward Dr. Kraus by virtue of reading his earlier book, *The Community of the Spirit*, as part of preparation for a series of Bible studies I was writing on the theme of *Christ's Peace*. In fact, in the bibliography of that book I recommended chapter four of *The Community of the Spirit*, "The Gospel of Peace," as one of the finest treatments of that subject. Thus, I came to this venture with only positive feelings. That is fortunate in that the reading of *Jesus Christ Our Lord* raised many questions in my mind.

Thirdly, by way of introduction, it may help to say a little more about my own theological background and perspective which will help others in evaluating my reflections. As indicated above, I represent the Reformed tradition. However, that tradition is also represented by figures as diverse as Karl Barth and Robert McAfee

Brown, on the one hand, and Cornelius Van Til and R. C. Sproul, on the other.

My own particular branch of that tradition is Dutch-American Reformed, which means that part of my theological heritage can be identified with names like Abraham Kuyper and Herman Bavinck of a past generation and more directly with contemporary theologians like G. C. Berkouwer and Hendrikus Berkhof. Unlike many of my Christian Reformed friends (our more conservative counterparts), however, I am not a true-blue Kuyperian, and unlike some of my Reformed Church in America friends, I am closer to Berkouwer than to H. Berkhof, although the latter is a good friend. My main problem with Berkhof, as with Kraus, is his attempting a Christology "from below" which results in something less than Chalcedonian orthodoxy. It may also be helpful to point out that while the New Testament scholar, Oscar Cullmann, was one of my mentors at the University of Basel, I regard his *Christology of the New Testament* problematic at certain points because of his functional approach, the very thing which appeals to Norman Kraus!

Having done graduate studies with Emil Brunner (in Japan) and Karl Barth, the latter being my *Doktorvater* at the University of Basel, I have naturally been influenced by both of them. I am neither Brunnerian nor Barthian, however, although I feel both have made important contributions to Christology. Nor am I a traditional Calvinist, for I am closer to Calvin himself than to the scholastic Calvinism represented by seventeenth-century orthodoxy. Since my doctoral dissertation was on *Calvin's Concept and Use of the Law*, I am not surprisingly more sensitive to Kraus's criticism of Calvin than to later Protestant scholasticism of which B. B. Warfield is an outstanding American example. (I read a lot of Warfield, along with Emil Brunner, as a seminary student). In fact, in a little book I wrote recently I try to clear up various misunderstandings concerning the Reformed tradition by moving behind what I regard as occasional Calvinistic aberrations by appealing to Calvin and the sixteenth-century Reformed confessions.[1] I think Dr. Kraus would resonate with some of my efforts.

I also consider myself an evangelical and feel at home with evangelical theologians like Donald Bloesch and Bernard Ramm. As a theological student, and early in my missionary career, I was fascinated by the question of the atonement and read widely in that area, particularly enjoying the works of James Denney, P.T. Forsyth, and Leon Morris (*The Apostolic Preaching of the Cross*, 1955). I also read the works of Vincent Taylor on the person and work of Christ (along with Warfield, Brunner, Berkouwer, and Donald Baillie, *God Was in Christ*, 1948).

I mention all this, both for the benefit of Dr. Kraus and for other participants in the consultation so that my subsequent comments will be understood in context. In addition, given this background and peculiar theological stance, it should already be apparent why I have difficulties with certain aspects of Kraus's Christology-- and also why I appreciate many other insights in this book.

Preliminary observations and questions

Kraus's purpose and methodology

In his preface, Kraus explains that he was motivated to write this Christology primarily for two reasons. His first motivation was to write a Christology which would reflect his experiences in non-western cultural contexts, particularly those of Asia and Africa. While my own experience overseas, apart from Western Europe, has been limited largely to Japan, living over 15 years in that country has made an indelible impact on my own thinking. Hence I appreciate very much Kraus's openness and sensitivity to these cultures and his attempt to relate to them. As we are learning from various liberation theologians--whether black, feminist, or Latin American--the gospel takes on new meaning when viewed from a different cultural perspective.[2]

Accordingly, it is refreshing to see Kraus examine how the language of self-disclosure functions in Hinduism and Buddhism (p. 117f.) and how the covenant concept breaks down in a Japanese context (p. 174f.).

Of particular interest is Kraus's handling of the shame (*haji*) concept which plays such a prominent role in Japanese society. As Kraus observes,

> In cultures where individuals find their self-identity and approval through inclusion in the group, exclusion and alienation from the group are the most dreaded results of wrong-doing. Shame experienced as feelings of embarrassment, unworthiness, and remorse follows the realization of wrongdoing. The biblical concept of reconciliation clearly speaks also to this kind of alienation which sin has caused (p. 181).

Consequently, for Christian witness to be effective in Japan, it must try to speak to this situation. The problem is that shame is primarily a societal concept. One feels shame only in relation to one's superiors. It is true at the highest level one can do something

which disgraces the country or the emperor, but since a transcendent
dimension is lacking in popular Japanese thought, one does not
reach the seriousness and depth of the biblical concepts of sin and
guilt.

The eminent Roman Catholic religious sociologist Joseph Spae,
who spent many years in Japan, believes that

> the gap between shame and sin, between a shame culture
> and a guilt culture, is not as wide as one might think. I
> believe that it is being filled in favor of a deeper conscious-
> ness of personal interior guilt, parallel to the progress of
> freedom from societal pressures toward a general accept-
> ance of personal responsibility.[3]

This, however, is a rather optimistic outlook, which is not confirmed by some of my Japanese friends. The impact of Buddhism,
and more recently Christianity, may have given a more religious
meaning to that word--and to that of *tsumi*, the word for sin which
connotes primarily a misdeed or crime--but shame (*haji*) is still basically a Confucian concept and hence suggests "a model of morality
understood not in terms of good and evil but of the noble and the
mean."[4]

For this reason I have reservations about Kraus's attempt to
identify shame and guilt in chapter 12. The Bible inevitably speaks
to both, but there is no biblical basis for equating shame with guilt.
Kraus points to Isaiah 6:1-5 and Luke 5:8; 7:6 and comments:
"Shame is a fundamental aspect of the moral response, but its full
ethical character depends upon an ethical perception of the *holy* one
in whose presence it feels defilement" (p. 206). It is precisely this
"ethical perception of the *holy* one" which is lacking in the Japanese
consciousness. Therefore, it seems to me, Kraus's understanding of
this notion differs fundamentally from the Japanese view.

Kraus distinguishes between shame and guilt, pointing to subjective and objective aspects of both, and contends that "the role of
the cross in reconciling us to God must be seen in broader terms as
an answer to both shame and guilt" (p. 207). Agreed, but when
Kraus goes on to assert that "the resolution of the shame problem...provides the context and paradigm for understanding the
resolution of guilt, not vice-versa" (p. 208), I must demur. I would
see shame as one aspect of the larger problem of sin and guilt, not
vice-versa.

What Kraus does here reminds me of Robert Schuller's
attempt to define sin as basically a lack of self-esteem. In fact,
Schuller's solution is that if "we focus on Jesus Christ, we shall dis-

cover a new theology, one that offers *salvation from shame* to self-esteem."[5] The similarities, I grant, are superficial, but in both cases I feel the root-problem is an underestimation of the nature and power of sin, partially due to an over-reaction against the Augustinian view.

A second motivation in writing *Jesus Christ Our Lord* was the attempt to write a Christology from a distinctly Anabaptist view-point, i.e, from a disciple's perspective (the subtitle) and as a "peace theology" (p. 17).

This gives to this Christology a special focus and flavor and makes it especially interesting for one outside this tradition. It also means that one can anticipate disagreements, especially when this distinctive point of view is accented, particularly in contrast to the Augustinian-Reformed Protestant tradition which I represent. However, I am attracted to the idea of doing theology from a disciple's perspective, even though I am not quite certain as to what this entails. When Kraus writes, "a disciple's theology will be oriented to a time and place rather than attempt a universal statement" (p. 17), I'm reminded of Karl Barth's statements to that effect concerning his monumental *Church Dogmatics*. And when Kraus adds, "And last, it will be oriented to the message and strategy of the church in making disciples of all nations" (p. 17), I recall Emil Brunner's goal of being a missionary theologian, which he too enacted when he resigned his position in Zurich in order to go to Japan in 1953.

So I find it difficult to discern what is unique or distinctively Mennonite about his approach. Kraus notes there is a "further explanation" in his essay "Toward a Theology for the Disciple Community" (p. 17), but I don't have access to that.

I also have some difficulty in determining precisely what an Anabaptist "peace theology" is, although some of the implications of that position are spelled out here. However, I am not sure whether some of the distinctive slants in this book are due so much to an Anabaptist "peace theology" or to Kraus's particular personalist, anti-metaphysical approach. Granted, there is cleavage between the so-called "biblical peace position" and mainline Protestantism; but when Kraus asserts, "A peace theology should be a cross and resurrection theology," no evangelical--whether Anglican, Lutheran, or Reformed--will take exception to that. Anglicans in particular might add the incarnation to that phrase and Pentecostals would want to add the Holy Spirit, but such an assertion in itself does not separate Mennonites from other Protestants except insofar as this is interpreted to imply pacifism.

The same would apply to the next assertion (in the Preface) that "Jesus Christ himself must be the 'Alpha and Omega' of a peace theology" (p. 17). This too would find ready acceptance among most

Protestant--and probably most Roman Catholic--theologians as well. The question, of course, is which Jesus Christ? Kraus hints at a special hermeneutical approach in this regard when he says that "Jesus himself is the normative criterion for theology" (p. 17), although again that statement by itself does not point to anything radical or distinctive. When he adds a few lines later, "We seek to understand God in light of Jesus" (p. 18), I can only point out that Barth would respond with a hearty "Amen" to that. Kraus may object to Barth's giving such great prominence to the Trinity in his prolegomena (*Church Dogmatics* I, 2), but one could hardly be more Christocentric than Karl Barth in one's approach to the whole theological enterprise. Note, for example, Barth's Christological approach to creation in Volume III of the *Church Dogmatics* (which, not so incidentally, many of Barth's admirers, including myself, find very problematic at points). Barth would concur with Kraus when he states that "inasmuch as Jesus is the 'Word of God' and the true 'image of God,' we interpret the Genesis story in the light of the revelation which has come in him" (p. 85).

Later (p. 85, n.5) Kraus indicates that his own approach is Christologically more radical than Luther's, although Luther saw all of the Old Testament as "the swaddling clothes and the manger in which Christ lies." I am curious as to what this means concretely. I have a nagging suspicion after reading this volume that it may mean a downplaying not only of the significance of the Old Testament foreshadowing of and witness to Christ, as found for example in Isaiah 53 and Daniel 7 (strangely ignored here), but also of the Old Testament as such. If there is this tendency or danger in such a Christological peace hermeneutic, then the warning of G. C. Berkouwer is apposite:

> One who begins by devaluating the Old Testament will, by some inner logic, end up depriving the New Testament of its value.... One who tosses out the Old Testament, though he still speaks with appreciation about the New, is bound like Harnack, to have an impoverished view of it too. Progression in the history of redemption from the old covenant to the new does not imply an elimination of the witness of the Old. The elimination of this source can only result in impoverishment.[6]

I do not mean to suggest that Kraus "tosses out the Old Testament," but it obviously does not play the role in his theology that it does in most Christologies. And when our author makes statements like the following, I am not reassured:

> The Old Testament...has great religious value as a guide and corrective to cross-cultural interpretations on the New Testament materials. But our point here is that it does not have final authority for interpreting the Christ event....(p. 85)

Granted, but what kind of authority does it have? Need one denigrate the authority of the Old Testament in order to establish its Christian significance?

So much for the methodological/hermeneutical principles of this work as stated in the preface. Thus far, it should be clear I have more questions than objections. Formally, at least, I do not see that we differ as much as Kraus seems to think, although there may be more here than meets the eye.

The not-so-hidden agenda

There is, however, a third motivation behind the writing of this work, although it is never stated as such, viz., the constant and consistent polemic against classical catholic orthodoxy as represented by the ancient creeds--(particularly Nicea and Chalcedon), the major reformers (particularly Luther and Calvin) and later Protestant orthodoxy (particularly the seventeenth century scholastics and their heirs such as B. B. Warfield and Loraine Boettner). (It should be noted that the latter has little or no standing even in the Reformed community and hence does not deserve even the little attention given to him by Kraus on p. 70.) Underlying much of this criticism is a strong antipathy to anything that smacks of a philosophical ontological approach.

This is sweeping judgment, but a perceptive reader of *Jesus Christ Our Lord* will recognize that this is no exaggeration. Here is only a sampling of the evidence:

> The Greek church fathers attempted to rationalize the New Testament witness to Jesus as the Son of God. They used the language of Greek dualistic metaphysics to interpret New Testament concepts such as 'Word of God' and 'Son of God' (p. 47).

> The individual texts are to be used as *witness* to the original revelational experience and not as normative theological pronouncements (p. 86; cf. 81).

Both Roman Catholic and Protestant orthodoxy have used the philosophical language of ontology to describe the unity of Jesus with the Father (p. 113).

The fact that the orthodox tradition has felt comfortable with the less personal language to ontological metaphysics is revealing in itself (p. 119).

Other examples could be given, but this should suffice to show the anti-metaphysical bias which runs through this book, although at one point we find the surprising statement: "Guilt is ontological, not merely legal" (p. 224)! As far as I can determine, this is the only case where "ontological" is not used in a pejorative sense.

In response to all this, I want to stress first of all that I am sympathetic with at least one aspect of these criticisms, viz., the anti-scholastic slants. Seventeenth-century scholasticism, based on an Aristotelian logic, has bedeviled Reformed theology far too long and continues to be the basis for one type of fundamentalist apologetics (e.g., the rationalism of the late Gordon Clark, influential philosopher in fundamentalist circles, and a contemporary theologian like Carl Henry). In my own denomination it was one of our Old Testament scholars, the late Lester J. Kuyper, who kept pressing the theologians of a past generation concerning their all too Greek notions of God?[7]

Kraus has clearly rejected Aristotle (and Plato). Fine, but where does this leave him? Wittingly or unwittingly we all operate with some metaphysics or ontology, even if we reject the traditional Greek forms. Kraus may object and claim that his functional approach is the antithesis to all ontologies, but I would maintain that even the most radical historicism is based on some view of reality.

Kraus appears to be operating with a type of personalist-historicist philosophy, although this is never made explicit. He suggests that this is a biblical way of thinking--particularly Hebraic, although he acknowledges Hellenistic influences within the Bible. In his antipathy to Greek metaphysics he comes close to repeating the once-popular Greek-Hebrew antithesis expounded by Thorleif Boman in his *Hebrew Thought Compared with Greek* (E.T. 1961). This kind of bifurcation is generally regarded as passe in biblical circles today, but Kraus seems to follow in this train (or is he closer to Harnack?) in rejecting out of hand the Greek fathers and the early Catholic creeds because they used Greek philosophical language.

I would concede that dogmatics or systematic theology has been overly influenced by Greek categories, one of the chief examples being the impassability of God. Hence, any notions that God could really "repent" of some action (L. Kuyper), could experience pain (K. Kitamori), or pathos (A. Heschel) were automatically ruled out and labeled heretical (Patripassianism). But are we to reject any theology tainted with Greek thought? Is everything Bultmann wrote invalid because he bought into Heidegger's philosophy? Or are we to reject totally Moltmann's theology of hope because he uses insights from Hegel and a Marxist philosopher, Ernst Bloch?

I belabor this point because I think that Kraus's rejection of Nicene-Chalcedonian Christology lands him in some metaphysical mist with serious consequences. More about that later.

One can reject an Aristotelian metaphysics and the rationalist scholasticism of the seventeenth-century orthodox fathers without rejecting a traditional Christology. A case in point is Emil Brunner, who still has something to say to us even though his theology has been eclipsed by Barth, Tillich, and more recently process and liberation theologians. Kraus must be aware of him since Brunner's theology was so influential in the U.S. in the post-war period (except in fundamentalist and right-wing Calvinistic circles where both Barth and he were rejected as dangerous exponents of a new modernism, e.g. C. Van Til).

The parallels between Brunner and Kraus are so many and so striking I am amazed that there is not a single reference to him. On page after page I wrote in the margins "a'la E. B." (e.g., pp. 34, 53, 105, 113, 116, 118), for Brunner, like Kraus, felt that the nemesis of much conservative Protestant theology was its objectivism, i.e., God was conceived of as an abstract object instead of a subject who communicates himself to us personally, above all in Jesus Christ. He too opposed a creedalism where faith is construed as a "bloss für wahr halten," simply believing that something is true. Utilizing the personalist philosophy of Husserl, the I-Thou approach of F. Ebner and M. Buber, and the existentialism of S. Kierkegaard, he tried to resolve the subject-object antithesis with his ideas of personal correspondence and truth as encounter. It should be noted that he also opposed the subjectivism of liberalism, particularly as represented by Schleiermacher, and its variant in pietism. This aspect of Brunner's theology is best expressed in his early programmatic work *Wahrheit als Begegnung* (1938), first published in English under the misleading title *The Divine-Human Encounter* (1943) and later reissued with a new preface under the title *Truth as Encounter*.[8]

I also have reservations about what I regard as excesses in Brunner's theology, but I cite him because he shares many of the concerns of Kraus (including a rejection of verbal inspiration and reservations about a literal virgin birth) but still maintains a high

Christology, not basically different from Nicea and Chalcedon, a fairly traditional view of the Trinity, similar to that of the Athanasian Creed, and an objective view of the atonement, unlike Dr. Kraus!

The point I am trying to make is that one may share many of Kraus's concerns--as I do--about the undue influence in theology of Greek philosophy, Aristotelian logic, and rationalistic scholasticism, and yet not throw out the baby with the bath water. This brings me to the two key issues to which I have alluded several times already: Kraus's Christology and his view of the atonement. Then I want to conclude by pointing out some of the things I found especially suggestive and helpful in this book.

Jesus Christ, truly God?

I shall not wait until the concluding section to acknowledge my debt to Norman Kraus for his fresh and challenging treatment of the humanity of Jesus. Like most theologians of orthodox/evangelical persuasion, not to mention lay people, it has always been easier to confess that Jesus Christ is truly God than to confess that he is truly human. Actually, the formal confession of both truths is easy enough; the difficulty begins when trying to spell out what his humanity entails. It is clear from the Gospel accounts that he hungered, became weary and angry, needed time to be alone and pray, and was limited in his knowledge of the future. Beyond that, however, like most conservative types, I was not ready to concede very much. Accordingly, my Jesus was not very human, for if he could not sin, I also concluded that he could not make a mistake and was also not liable to most of the passions, weaknesses, and frailties that plague all ordinary mortals. What one Dutch critic (A. van de Beek) has said of the earlier Karl Barth's Christology could also be said of me: "Jesus is so much on the side of God that his humanity is almost dwarfed into insignificance."[9]

Consequently, I found chapter three, "The Man, Christ Jesus," one of the most interesting and challenging chapters in the book. I would only add to his opening statement, that emphasizing Jesus' humanity is important not only for a discipleship theology but also for a biblical Christology (p. 63). I also concur in his two basic convictions: 1) "that God is a self-giving Creator who fully identifies with us in our need," and 2) "that our humanity finds its true fulfillment in this one who is the prototypical 'image of God'" (p. 64). Kraus says later, "The characteristics of that image are meekness, obedience, forgiveness, and servanthood--true righteousness and holiness' (Eph. 4:23-24)" (p. 66). To that I would also add compassion; for the chief attribute of Jesus in his response to those in need, whether physical or spiritual, was compassion (see Matt. 9:36; 14:14; 15:32, and note how the key word in the parables of the good Samaritan and the prodigal son is compassion--Lk. 10:33; 15:20. Cf. the Samuel and Sugden quote on p. 69).

I also can concur with Kraus's insistence on "a full personal identification which involves Jesus in the existential frustration and dilemmas which we face as we attempt to obey the voice of God" (p. 69). But I must confess I get uneasy when on the basis of texts like Hebrews 5:8 ("Jesus *learned* to obey") Kraus concludes, "All this certainly infers that he was vulnerable to making mistakes, which, of course, are not the same as sins" (p. 70). Also, when Jesus is described as "fallible," I would want some concrete illustrations of that fallibility before making a firm decision concerning that notion.

I have more serious reservations about Kraus's handling of the virgin birth. Granted, sometimes in conservative circles it has been misunderstood and misused (also in Roman Catholic theology) to provide biological proof of Jesus' divinity or to guarantee his sinlessness. The virgin birth is indeed a miracle, and miracles, as Kraus observes, "remain faith data." The problem arises, he adds, "when the virgin birth is considered a rational or empirical explanation for the deity of Jesus" (p. 75).

However, why does Kraus (like Emil Brunner) make so much of the fact that the virgin birth "plays virtually no theological role" in the rest of the New Testament (pp. 74-5)? Why does he scorn a "literalistic hermeneutic" (p. 76) which wants to take the accounts at face value? Can one not hold to the literal, historical fact of the virgin birth and still be "aware of the multi-dimensional possibilities for meaning in such a passage" (p. 79)? Or can we only find meaning or significance in the account by denying its historicity as Hans Küng and many modern scholars do? The three theological points Kraus makes on page 78 are all valid ones, but the crux of the matter is whether "the virgin birth is the way in which God the pre-existent Son came into human existence without a change of divine substance" (p. 76). It is precisely this which Kraus appears to deny on the grounds that this represents Greek ontological thinking.

This brings us to the major issue of the first section of the book, viz., in what sense Jesus is the son of the Father (title of chapter four) and the self-disclosure of God (title of chapter five).

At the beginning of chapter five our author raises several key questions: "Is Jesus Christ the authentic representation of God's authority and power? Did he come from God? Is he the 'way' to God? In short, is he truly the self-disclosure of God" (p. 103)? The second question is the critical one, for one could answer the others affirmatively and still stop short of a historic Christology.

Kraus does not hesitate to speak of Jesus' deity, but his definitions of that deity are unusual and hence leave me perplexed. For
example, he says that "when we speak of Jesus' deity...we are saying
that the God who at best was dimly and inadequately known through
creation and law reveals the fuller dimensions of his character to us
in Jesus" (p. 103). Fine, but does this only mean that Jesus is a
greater prophet than Moses? He goes on to say that "when we speak
of Christ as deity...we are saying that God is the kind of God who
relates to the universe, human beings, and history like [sic] he
related to us in Christ" (p. 103). This is an unusual way of describing
Christ's deity, and that is perhaps why I am unclear as to what Kraus
is trying to say here.

The key issue, in any case, is the incarnation, and more particularly the question of the preexistence of Christ. Here I am surprised
that Kraus does not even allude to the recent debate about "the myth
of God incarnate" (the title of a book published by seven British
theologians in 1977). Interaction with this volume and subsequent
reactions would have sharpened the issue.

Kraus, in any case, acknowledges that in John, in particular, "in
order to underscore Jesus' identity with this eternal reality [in John
1:1] the language of eternal existence is applied to him." According
to John, Jesus "shared God's eternal glory and he was sent from the
bosom of the Father." As Kraus adds, "John's language is most
explicit" (p. 104). Indeed it is, but then Kraus, consistent with his
anti-ontological bias and rejection of the Chalcedonian formula,
makes the astounding statement, "It seems clear that this is not an
ontological statement about the existence of the human Jesus before
his birth, but rather an emphatic identification of the Word spoken
in Jesus with the eternal Word" (p. 104).

This statement must be taken together with the footnote relating to an earlier statement cited above: "The Word 'preexistence'
itself does not occur in the Bible or in the major creeds, and we need
to be careful about what it does and does not mean. It does not
mean that Jesus existed before his birth" (p. 105, n. 2).

I must confess that I am baffled by these statements. Either we
have here a tautology, a Trinitarian confusion, or a heresy--or Kraus
is too subtle for my comprehension! If the first--a tautology--Kraus
is merely saying the obvious, i.e., that the *man* Jesus of Nazareth
could not exist before he was born. If the second, then Kraus is
drawing too sharp a distinction between Jesus of Nazareth and the
eternal son of God, the Logos, who became incarnate in Jesus of
Nazareth, the child born of the virgin Mary. If the third, then Kraus
is simply denying--as did the authors of *The Myth of God Incarnate*--

that Jesus is in fact the eternal son of God, the third person of the Trinity. I look forward to the discussion which should clear up this crucial question. The answer, I suspect, is found in the second and third paragraphs of the footnote on page 105 where Kraus pits an allegedly biblical view of preexistence over against the Chalcedonian view that Jesus Christ as the third person of the Trinity existed from all eternity. It seems to me that it is simply perverse to suggest that in the classic Christology of the church we have "the hypostatization of a Platonic ideal or the mythology of Hellenism" (p. 105 n. 2).

This is not to say that the Chalcedonian formula is the last word on the subject. It does rely on sophisticated Greek philosophical terminology because those were the terms of the debate which it was trying to solve. It is also largely negative, for it does not solve the problem so much as set the boundaries beyond which one cannot go and still remain faithful to the biblical evidence. The framers of the formula would no doubt have been the first to admit that we are dealing here with a paradox, a mystery. But that does not mean it doesn't make sense, even if we concede with William Temple, "If any man says that he understands the relation of Deity to humanity in Christ, he only makes it clear that he does not understand at all what is meant by an incarnation."[10] Davis concedes that the New Testament never makes the precise statement that "Jesus Christ is truly God and truly man,"

> hence these words can never take on scriptural authority for Christians. Nevertheless, centuries of Christian tradition attest to the adequacy of these words as best formulating the Christian understanding of the person of Jesus as he was historically encountered by the disciples, as he is read about in the Scriptures, and as he is spiritually encountered by believers today (p.224).

I am not averse to Kraus's attempt to try a fresh approach and use personalistic language rather than Greek philosophical terms to resolve the paradox. The language of communion, of "identity of selfhood" (p. 113), and social psychology can be useful in trying to rethink the relation of the "persons" of the Trinity. Perhaps "the ultimate metaphysical sphere is best understood in personal metaphors of self rather than the physical [?!] metaphor of spirit" (p. 115, n. 13).

However, when Jesus' unity with the Father is expressed only in terms of him representing "God's inner character and attitude toward us" (p. 117), I cannot refrain from wondering whether this does justice to the New Testament portrayal of Jesus' relation to

God. The same applies to the following assertion:

> When we think of Jesus' relation to God as the personal
> unity of self-identity, we have a paradigm for our own rela-
> tion as children of God. His union with God *was given* to
> him in history. It was his as the gift of selfhood--his own
> personal identity as God's Son. His deity was not a
> preexistent divine substance which was transported to earth
> and combined with human flesh and rationality to produce
> an independent divine-human being. It was *God's work* in
> and through Jesus. (p. 117)

The last statement is a caricature of the orthodox position, but
Kraus may feel this is necessary to justify his own reductionist
Christology. This may sound harsh, but I agree with Bernard Ramm
in his judgment that "a reductionist Christology is any Christology
which comes measurably short of historic Christology."[11]

Given his Christology "from below" and functional approach,
Kraus affirms as much as is possible of Jesus. He can even say
"Jesus is the true and living image of God and actually participates in
the divine reality which he represents" (p. 96). Moreover, by virtue
of titles such as "Lord" and "King," "Jesus is identified with God's
purpose, power, authority, and personal character" (p. 94). These
are strong statements, but they fall short of affirming the great
Christmas message that the child of the virgin is "Emmanuel...God
with us" (Luke 2:23. It is ironic that this key text for Karl Barth--he
cites it again and again in *Evangelical Theology: An Introduction*--is
not cited once by Kraus).

Toward a fully biblical doctrine of the atonement

The atonement, like the incarnation, is a mystery better
believed and adored than analyzed and explained. Yet the task of
the theologian is to try to make sense out of the biblical data and
present it as meaningfully as possible. Kraus does that in a clear and
creative fashion, although again I have a host of questions.

I feel very comfortable with his transition chapter seven on
Christ as prophet, priest, and king, a schema introduced by Calvin
and now common in most Protestant dogmatics. Although Kraus
often fails to do justice to Calvin, here I must concede the validity of
his criticism that Calvin--and the Reformers generally--spiritualized
the notion of Christ's kingship and didn't do justice to his prophetic
office. When it comes to the atonement, however, I note that Kraus
makes "the kingship-lordship of Jesus the primary soteriological

category" (p. 132). This surprises me because normally the priestly or sacrificial aspect of Christ's death dominates discussions of his redemptive work. There is no question that "most of Jesus' teaching focuses on this reign of God" (p. 138). And Kraus rightly emphasizes a point missing in many traditional theologies and studies of the atonement, viz., that Jesus' "ministry of forgiveness is a part of this inauguration of the kingdom of God. His *salvation* activity as the Messiah was already begun in his earthly ministry" (p. 138; cf. pp. 166 and 167, n.6). This motif is totally missing, for example, in Emil Brunner's classic *The Mediator.* By way of contrast, Theodore R. Clark has written a book on the atonement entitled, *Saved by His Life* (Macmillan, 1959), based on Romans 5:10b.

Nevertheless, even the gospels focus on the final week of Jesus' life, precisely because they see the passion, death, and resurrection of Christ as the focal point and climax of his life and ministry. When one takes into consideration a key text in the synoptic gospels (Mark 10:45), the sacrificial imagery in John's Gospel (1:29,36), and above all the frequent references to the blood of Christ, his death as an expiation for our sins (Rom. 3:25 [*hilasterion*]; 1 John 2:2; 4:10 [*hilasmos*]; Heb. 2:17), and the theme of the heavenly priesthood of Christ (Heb. 4:14-5, 7-10), much of which Kraus notes in various contexts (see pp. 181-3), it is clear that sacrificial/priestly metaphors are prominent in describing the redemptive significance of the death of Christ. He also notes that "both the ransom metaphor and the victor metaphor are used in the New Testament" (p. 182); but earlier he had commented that "metaphors of the battlefield or law courts must play a secondary and circumscribed role" in the interpretation of the cross (p. 168).

Quite apart from Gustav Aulen's analysis in *Christus Victor* (which I believe is one-sided), I think one should take seriously the motif of conflict and the victory over the powers of sin, death, and the devil in Christ's death and resurrection (for texts see pp. 185-6). Aulen wants to make this "the" theory of the atonement. In this he is wrong, but I wouldn't describe this metaphor as "secondary" either. Nor would I say that of law court imagery, if by that one includes the concept of justification which has forensic overtones, especially in Romans 4, which Kraus strangely ignores in his discussion of justification (pp. 179-181).

I am also convinced that a biblical portrayal of the significance of Christ's death must include Abelard's positive affirmations that the incarnation, life, and death of Christ are the supreme revelation of the love of God and should evoke from us a response of faith and love. ("Love so amazing so divine, demands my soul, my life, my all".)

To all of this Kraus makes his own special contribution by using personal metaphors, particularly that of the parent-child analogy, "for illuminating God's way with his children" (p. 161, cf. 168). In this connection Kraus shows how God's unconditional *agape*-love creates personhood and "gives us ultimate self-worth because God gives himself to us" (p. 165).

But the critical question remains, "Why the cross?" and here I am not altogether satisfied with Kraus's answers. One answer is that "the divine necessity of Jesus' death is inherent in the nature of God's love on the one hand, and the nature of human sin on the other" (p. 164). "Therefore, given the nature and goal of love and the character of human sin, the death of Christ was both inevitable and necessary for the advancement of the kingdom of God in the world" (p. 168).

In both of these quotations sin is mentioned, but sin for Kraus is largely depicted in subjective terms: a broken relationship, fears, hostility, alienation, although "death is its ultimate weapon and power" (167). Such a description of sin is preferable to the traditional idea of sin as merely the breaking of a law. But there is also a corporate, objective aspect to sin, a great barrier which separates us from a holy, loving God. This is implied in the necessity of a reconciliation between God and humanity, a barrier which appears to exist on the side of God as well as human beings. Here is where Kraus and I apparently disagree, particularly in our exegesis of two key passages, Romans 3:21-26 and 2 Corinthians 5:18-21.

Concerning the former passage he writes, "These verses do not necessarily teach a change in God's manner of dealing with sin but rather a clarification of his action which changes the subjective situation of mankind" (p. 161, n.1). This is a telling comment, for although God does not change in his *attitude* toward humanity, there is evidence to the effect that his *manner* or way of *dealing* with humanity changes. A key text here is Romans 3:25-26. Kraus acknowledges this, but makes the above remark in connection with the fact that God has always "required a faith relationship" (v. 25--"to be received by faith"). However, he ignores the critical issue in the last part of verse 25, and especially verse 26.

> This was to show God's righteousness, because in his divine forbearance he had passed over sins; it was to prove at the present time that he himself is righteous [or just] and that he justifies him who has faith in Jesus.

The point here is not only that "the true nature of his [God's] eternal righteousness has been disclosed in Christ" (p. 161, n.1), but that God can now forgive sins and be true to his own inmost ethical character, something that was not possible before. The implication is that God could not justify sinners prior to the death of Christ and be truly just/righteous. This is why he had to "pass over" or "over-look" (NEB) former sins--i.e., leave them "unpunished" (see Jerusalem Bible and NIV translations), a point also made by Paul in two of his speeches recorded in Acts 14:16 and 17:30. Thanks to the "propitiatory sacrifice" (Cranfield's translation of *hilasterion*) of Jesus Christ on the cross, the tension between the justice and mercy of God in dealing with sinners is resolved. C. E. B. Cranfield, the premier interpreter of Romans, interprets this key verse (Rom. 3:26) in this way:

> The words afford an insight into the innermost meaning of the cross as Paul understands it. For God to have forgiven men's sin lightly--a cheap forgiveness which would have implied that moral evil does not matter very much--would have been altogether unrighteous, a violation of his truth, and profoundly unmerciful and unloving toward men, since it would have annihilated their dignity as persons morally accountable.... The forgiveness accomplished through the cross is the costly forgiveness, worthy of God, which, so far from condoning man's evil, is, since it involves nothing less than God's bearing the intolerable burden of that evil him-self in the person of his own dear Son, the disclosure of the fullness of God's hatred of man's evil at the same time as it is its real and complete forgiveness.[12]

What is at stake here is not simply the interpretation of one verse, but the objective character of the atonement. Does Christ's death make a difference to God as well as to human beings? Is the situation different for God as well as for us after the reconciliation effected by Christ on the cross? I believe we must answer in the affirmative and interpret 2 Corinthians 5:19ff. and Romans 5:19ff. to mean that prior to Christ's saving death we existed under the wrath as well as the love of God, that the objective situation of humanity is radically different before and after the cross, quite apart from any response on our part.

Leon Morris cites P. T. Forsyth in this connection: "God's feel-ing for us never needed to be changed. But God's treatment of us, God's practical relation to us--that had to change" (from *The Work of Christ*, p. 105). Then he adds: "God's love for us remained unchanged throughout the process of reconciliation.... God's love never varied. But the atonement wrought by Christ means that men are no longer treated as enemies (as their sin deserves), but as friends. God has reconciled himself."[13]

I suspect the notion of God "reconciling himself" may be repugnant to Dr. Kraus, given his apparent rejection of the traditional evangelical understanding of the atonement, but I believe a good case can be made for this understanding on the basis of the two passages cited above, viz., 2 Cor. 5:19ff. and Romans 5:9ff. His strong reaction to Anselm and classical Protestantism (155 f.) indicates that we are at odds here. In response I would like to make the following three points:

1. There is, I feel, a basic truth in the Anselmic view, viz., the objective character of the atonement, but no one, as far as I know, follows Anselm's theory in its details, e.g., his particular idea of satisfaction, the role of the devil, merit, etc. Above all, those who owe much to Anselm--from Luther and Calvin, James Denney and P. T. Forsyth, to Emil Brunner and Karl Barth--would emphasize much more the love of God as the primary source of our reconciliation and the fact that there is no tension between the Father and the Son in effecting that reconciliation.

2. It is simply false to suggest, as Kraus does, that Calvin and Protestant orthodoxy are simply following Esdras and his Jewish view of God as a just lawgiver (p. 153 ff.). Moreover, it is not fair to Calvin and the Reformed theologians who followed him to assert that "they defined justice to mean punitive justice, that is, giving equivalent violent punishment for violence committed" (p. 155).[14]

3. This is not simply a matter of a Mennonite peace approach to the atonement versus a traditional Reformed or orthodox view. The basic question is how this peace or reconciliation with God was achieved (see Rom. 5:1,11; Eph. 2:13ff.). The traditional way of answering this question is in terms of a substitutionary atonement, a term inimical to many scholars--and to Kraus, since he identifies it with "the penal substitutionary theory" where allegedly God's "love is circumcised by justice" (p. 156).

This accusation could hardly be made of Karl Barth with his profound view of God's sovereign grace; yet Barth's view of the atonement can simply be described as "Christ in our place."[15] Nor could it be directed against the English Methodist New Testament scholar, Vincent Taylor, who spent much of his life studying this theme. Taylor too taught in effect a substitutionary view of the atonement even though he didn't use the word. The "three characteristic aspects of Christ's saving deed," he says, "are that it is vicarious, representative [by which he means substitutionary], and sacrificial."[16] Nor could this same accusation be made of a scholar in the liberal tradition, John Knox, long-time professor of New

Testament at Union Seminary in New York. Commenting on
Romans 2:25, he writes:

> A price must be paid; a penalty must be suffered; a sacrifice
> must be offered.... Paul undoubtedly finds in the life and
> death of Christ the indispensable atoning sacrifice.[17]

That is it in a nutshell. It seems to me nothing less than this is
required by two key texts: "For our sake he [God] made him [Christ]
to be sin who knew no sin, so that in him we might become the
righteousness of God" (Rom. 5:21): and "Christ redeemed us from
the curse of the law, having become a curse for us...." (Gal. 2:13). If
these two texts don't suggest a penal substitutionary theory (rejected
by Kraus, 156), then their words have lost all meaning.

Instead, Kraus sees the cross as a symbol of "God's solidarity
with us even in our sinfulness" (p. 157) and cites passages like
Romans 8:3, Galatians 4:4-5; 2 Corinthians 5:21, and Hebrews 2:14-
18 in support of his thesis. "God is justified by an incarnation which
finds its consummation in the cross, and not by a legal transaction
which took place on the cross" (p. 157). I don't want to quibble
about words, and hence will concede that what we have in the cross
is far more than a "legal transaction," but it clearly involves God's
justice or righteousness (as we saw in Rom. 3:26), as well as the law
(Gal. 4:4-5) and a curse (Gal. 3:13). So I am willing to concede
Kraus's point as long as he does justice to such biblical motifs as
God's holiness, wrath, law, and curse, as well as his love, mercy, and
grace. But I don't see that the notion of solidarity--at least as Kraus
develops it--does justice to these realities.

Instead Kraus's view of the atonement looks more like a
process than a once-for-all act. Granted, the atonement is not com-
pleted, in a sense, until there is the response of faith. The reconciliation must be received (2 Cor. 5:20); and Christ's high priestly ministry continues (Heb. 7:25; 8:1ff.). But what are we to make of Kraus's
idea that God's act of solidarity in Jesus Christ represents God's
work as "a patient and loving creator who continues to complete
what he has begun" (p. 157)? Thereby God "continues to sustain and
'save,' or recreate it even in its perversity" (p. 157).

God has indeed never ceased his work of creation, but it seems
to me that Kraus confuses creation and redemption even when both
are broadly conceived. Redemption, in the last analysis, is an act of
re-creation, but I still find the following statements highly theoretical:

The incarnation culminating in the cross and resurrection

reveals to us the way in which God is at work finishing his
creation. In the face of human failure and evil it is the
process of vicarious death and resurrection. ...it is a process
of re-creation, that is, of reforming the deviant and restor-
ing that which what has been prostituted by sin. (p.158,
italics added)

If this were a description of *sanctification*, I would be satisfied,
but as an explanation of how God reconciled the world to himself I
find this strangely vague and unsatisfying. Later (in chapter nine)
Kraus searches for "objectivity" in personal metaphors such as the
parent-child analogy (p. 160ff.). His four examples (p. 162ff.) are
helpful illustrations, but are no more than that. In subsequent chapters some good points are made about "salvation as the renewal of
the image of God" (title of chapter 11), but again I would point out
that this is the *goal* of our salvation, not salvation itself.

Finally, in chapter 13, the question is asked, "How does Jesus'
solidarity with us in our shameful condition effect our salvation" (p.
218)? In this context Kraus will speak of substitution and a vicarious
self-sacrifice but these terms are not employed in the traditional, and
I would say, biblical sense, for "this is not the substitution of illegal
penalty which pays our debt to God's justice. It is rather the substitution of total identification which accepts responsibility for all the
group. He took our place including the consequences of this identification" (p. 219). Then he cites 2 Corinthians 5:21, but it is
questionable as to whether this is the meaning of the text.

What, then, does this solidarity with us in guilt mean? In short,
that "fully living among us as one of us and on our behalf, Jesus obli-
gated himself to live completely under the authority of God, fulfilling
the covenant responsibly ... even though it inevitably meant that he
would suffer the full consequences of our guilty alienation, namely,
death" (p. 226).

Some of these statements bear some resemblance to classical
biblical motifs, but I have the impression that Kraus is quite
deliberately saying something different even when he uses language
like "substitution" and "vicarious." This impression is confirmed in
the four points that are made in the conclusion of this chapter.
Jesus' death only *exposes* sin and *demonstrates* not God's justice but
only that "the true righteousness of love, [is] a love which creates the
new moral possibility by the gracious removal of the offense through
unlimited self-giving." And finally, as in Abelard, "in the mystery of
love this revelation of true righteousness moves us to repentance and
reunion with God..." (p. 227).

The discriminating reader will recognize that this is a far cry from the classical or evangelical understanding of the atonement. Kraus may be quite willing to acknowledge this, arguing that the classic or evangelical view does not do justice to the Scriptures. My contention is that, whatever the weaknesses may be of the traditional view, this view corresponds better to the New Testament portrayal than Kraus's. What we have in Kraus, I believe, are variations on themes promulgated earlier by people like McLeod Campbell (*The Nature of the Atonement*, 1856) and Horace Bushnell (*The Vicarious Sacrifice*, 1866).

Campbell the Scot and Bushnell the American differed in many ways

> but what they said about the atonement was fundamentally the same--the redemption that God offers us must be seen in terms that are consistent with God's own nature, in terms of God's love revealed in the life and death of Jesus Christ. Whether you describe it as 'vicarious confession' or as 'vicarious sacrifice,' it implies the same, an obedience to death in which we are called to participate.[18]

I regret that I have felt it necessary to focus on what are for me problematic or questionable aspects of Kraus's treatment of the atonement, for there is much here that is challenging and worthy of consideration. Unfortunately, in reacting against the traditional notions of the substitutionary atonement, especially in its penal form, he rejects that which I believe is biblical along with unfortunate cultural accretions. Would that he had recognized that it is not a matter of either/or but both the insights of the traditional view along with the new insights provided by social psychology and recent biblical studies are valid.

If he had taken this tack, he could have asserted along with the Baptist missionary theologian Robert H. Culpepper that R. W. Dale and Karl Barth were right in affirming that God in Christ has borne our sins and has endured the penalty rather than inflicting it. Such statements, says Culpepper, are biblical and true. "And yet," he adds, much in the manner of Kraus,

> we do not grasp the atonement in its most vital aspect until we go beyond the categories of law to interpret the atonement in terms of Christ's sympathetic identification with sinners. The reason is that we are not dealing with abstract entities such as law or justice or punishment or even love, but with personal relations--God's relation to man and man's relation to God.[19]

Much of what Kraus says about the atonement is suggestive and helpful, but the impact is mitigated--at least for this reader--because, unlike Culpepper, R. Wallace, R. Paul, and others, he rejects too much of the old in order to say something new.

Challenging insights

The final and most positive part of my response to Kraus's *Jesus Christ Our Lord* must be the shortest due to the unseemly length of this evaluation. Fortunately, I have already indicated at several points my appreciation for various insights. For example, the basic thrust of the book is challenging and helpful, viz., to write a Christology from a fresh perspective which includes Anabaptist and Asian insights along with the results of recent biblical and theological investigations. Although I did not find the peace theology motif as distinctive as I had anticipated, there were still many points where I was challenged to pause and re-evaluate my own Reformed position due to Kraus's criticisms or suggestions.

As noted earlier, Kraus's depiction of the humanity of Jesus is in many ways compelling and persuasive. Also, despite my misgivings about his view of the Trinity, particularly the preexistence of Christ, there is much to be said for Kraus's personal or social categories to describe Christ's relation to God such as "identity of selfhood." The refusal to separate the cross and the resurrection (pp. 88-91) in the accomplishment of our redemption is another important point overlooked in many treatments of the theme. Moreover, for a Reformed theologian it is especially gratifying to see how Kraus stresses and utilized the covenant theme (p. 174ff.). In this connection I also appreciated the kingdom motif, but would demur that "most traditional Protestant interpretations ... equate the kingdom with the invisible church" (p. 138). It is simply not true that for Calvin the church is "without political prerogatives or social mandate" (p. 139). How can one say that in view of the famous last chapter in the *Institutes* (IV.20) on civil government? And what about Bucer's classic, *De Regno Christi* (1550), which is virtually a theological economic-political treatise?

I liked the emphasis on the goal and the fruits of the atonement, viz., the renewal of creation, the restoration of the image of God, and the new dignity gained thereby (pp. 158, 165, 187ff.). In part two a unique contribution to the understanding of sin and its ramifications is the treatment of shame in relation to guilt.

I especially appreciated the last chapter and the stress on

koinonia or participation in Christ (p. 236) as a basic motif in our appropriation of Christ's salvation. Philippians 3:10 has long been a favorite text of mine, so I readily identify with this emphasis. Kraus's understanding of repentance or conversion (pp. 239f.) is surprisingly close to that of Calvin (see the *Institutes*, III.3) and the Reformed fathers (see Heidelberg Catechism, questions 88-90). Finally, the focus on solidarity with Christ in his mission (p. 241f.) is a theme which warms the cockles of this former missionary's heart, although I wonder what Kraus means when he says that we are not to *"prejudge* the world to destruction" (p. 244, underlining mine).

But I can only say "Amen" to Kraus's conclusion where we are urged to "allow our minds to be renewed in his [Christ's] likeness, take up his style as our own, and participate in his mission [as] under his lordship our lives take on new direction, integration, and purpose" (pp. 244-5).

Endnotes

1. See *On Being Reformed* (New York: Reformed Church Press, second edition, 1988).

2. Cf. the recent book by a young Presbyterian missionary theologian, Daniel J. Adams, professor of theology at Hanil Seminary in Korea: *Cross-Cultural Theology: Western Reflections in Asia* (Atlanta: John Knox Press, 1987).

3. *Japanese Religiosity* (Tokyo: Oriens Institute for Religious Research, 1971), 105.

4. Tetsuro Watsuji, a prominent Japanese philosopher, cited in Spae, *ibid.*, 104.

5. Robert Schuller, *Self-Esteem: The New Reformation* (Waco: Texas, 1982), 39, italics mine.

6. *The Person of Christ* (Grand Rapids: Eerdmans, E. T. 1954), 151-2.

7. Kuyper, "The Suffering and Repentance of God" in *The Scripture Unbroken* (Grand Rapids: Eerdmans, 1978). Cf. the essay by Hendrikus Berkhof, "The (Un) Changeability of God," which builds on L. Kuyper's work in a festschrift for the latter: *Grace Upon Grace*, edited by James I. Cook (Grand Rapids: Eerdmans, 1973). In this essay Berkhof concludes a survey of various ways of thinking of God with the trenchant statement, "In its doctrine of God, theology will always drift about between Aristotle and Hegel," (p. 25). The process theologians, currently so popular in more liberal circles, fall into the latter camp.

8. Philadelphia: Westminster, 1964.

9. From Klaas Runia, *The Present-Day Christological Debate* (Downers Grove, IL.: Inter-Varsity Press, 1984), 191.

10. Cited by Stephen T. Davis in his helpful essay, "Is 'truly God and truly man' coherent?" in *Christian Scholar's Review*, IX.3 (1980), 215.

11. *An Evangelical Christology. Ecumenic and Historic* (Nashville: Thomas Nelson, 1985), 196.

12. *Romans: A Shorter Commentary* (Grand Rapids: Eerdmans 1985/7), 75.

13. *The Apostolic Preaching of the Cross* (London: Tyndale Press, 1955), 220.

14. For a recent Reformed presentation of the atonement I would recommend Ronald S. Wallace, *The Atoning Death of Christ* (Westchester, SC: Crossway Books, 1981). A well-known Scottish Calvin scholar, Wallace spent the latter part of his career teaching theology at Columbia Theological Seminary. He accepts the traditional Protestant position but deepens and broadens it with later insights from people like F. D. Maurice, Karl Heim, McLeod Campbell, and Donald Baillie.

15. See especially the section in IV.1 of the *Church Dogmatics* entitled "The Judge Judged in Our Place," 211ff.

16. *The Cross of Christ* (London: Macmillan, 1956), 90.

17. *Interpreter's Bible*, vol. 9 (Nashville: Abingdon Press, 1954) 433-4.

18. Robert S. Paul, *The Atonement and the Sacraments* (London: Hodder & Stoughton, 1961), 161. Cf. his treatment of R. C. Moberly's concept of "vicarious

penitence" in his *Atonement and Personality*, 1901, pp. 162ff., and Hastings Rashdall's *The Idea of Atonement in Christian Theology*, 1901, pp. 170ff. Kraus echoes many of the concerns and ideas of these authors, who are Presbyterian, Anglican, and Congregational. Hence I do not find his slants on this theme peculiarly Anabaptist, for the most part.

19. *Interpreting the Atonement* (Grand Rapids: Eerdmans, 1966), 144.

CHAPTER 8
REPLY TO INTERPRETATIONS AND CRITICISMS

C. Norman Kraus

I have chosen to organize responses to my interlocutors according to major issues that they have raised rather than to treat each critique separately. From their differing perspectives--biblical, historical, theological, pastoral, and missiological--some of the same issues have been raised. Further, I have chosen not to reply to or explain questions about use of words such as "historical," "myth," etc., some of which I responded to verbally at the consultation. Rather, I want to take this chance to discuss at greater length some questions of methodology, the relation of contemporary theology to the creedal tradition, and several doctrinal definitions which are basic to my approach.

I am deeply grateful for the serious way in which my critics have read my book. They have affirmed much of what I have written. In some cases where they seemed to feel that they were disagreeing or correcting my position, it seemed to me that we were in fact in agreement. In other cases differing assumptions, definitions and methodology emerged. It is to these that I wish to direct my response. Where possible I will attempt to identify the person or persons who have raised the issue.

Methodological Considerations

I consider systematic theology to be essentially a hermeneutical discipline, and not a speculative one. This means that one begins with the biblical text as the basic document and attempts to transpose it into a new cultural context. This involves more than literal translation. In the words of Fumitaka Matsuoka, it requires a "reconceptualization." In the language of the translator we may refer to this as finding a "dynamic equivalent" for the original cultural expression. In this respect I have exercised more freedom than the hermeneutic of verbal inerrancy might allow, but it has been my intention to honor the authority of Scripture in this process.

Second, it means that one does not use the text to elicit further "supernatural" theological information which is not clearly stated or implied in it. In this respect I have been much more reserved than traditional orthodoxy. Orthodox theologians explicitly assumed that the Bible is a sourcebook for rational theological information which has been supernaturally revealed. They freely used syllogistic logic, or "speculation," to gain new information which was not explicit in Scripture itself. They held that the rational validity of the logical process ("science") guaranteed that such extensions were "*scriptural* truth." The results of such speculative extensions have been so thoroughly integrated into modern evangelicalism that to question the biblical warrant for some of these doctrines is in itself quite threatening to some.

My "hermeneutics of suspicion" may at first seem like a simple espousal of the old liberalism since I do question some of the orthodox theological definitions. But my reason for avoiding rational, metaphysical speculation differs fundamentally from that of the liberal theologians.

Liberalism established a rational procedure of its own which it applied to the text of Scripture. Only that which could pass the test of human reason was to be accepted as "revelation." This was quite explicit in its earliest deistic form. Later forms of liberal thought modified the rational and empirical tests used to authenticate Scripture, but the hallmark of liberalism and modernism has always been their reliance on the human reason. Thus liberal theology has tended to move away from the biblical text and to ground its "truth" on common sense, or more rational and scientific norms.

In contrast to such liberal assumptions and methodology, I think that theology as a hermeneutical discipline should begin with the definitive self-revelation of God in Christ as it has come to us in the biblical tradition.

This means that theology has two foci. First there is the original context of revelation to which the biblical text bears witness. Then there are the various contemporary contexts into which this message is to be transplanted. Biblical theology seeks to make clear the historical cultural context and message of the Bible. Contemporary contextual theology, sometimes called "systematic theology," attempts to translate that meaning across cultural boundaries into contemporary settings. For this reason methodological questions, both exegetical and theological, have a special importance for our discussion.

A number of methodological issues have been raised by my reviewers which need clarification. Mel Schmidt, while basically agreeing with my position, thinks that my work is definitely not "from a disciple's perspective," i.e., one accessible to the non-scholarly disciple, as I claim. Another of my pastoral reviewers also has raised the same objection. Here I need to point out that I do not consider "from a disciple's perspective" to be the same as "in a popular layperson's style."

My approach is from a "disciple's perspective" in the sense that I try to begin with the historically observed Jesus ("from below") and allow the convictions about his identity to emerge just as they did for the first disciples. And secondly, it is meant in the sense that the proper goal of theology is to stimulate and guide discipleship rather than to answer speculative questions about God and Christ. Disciples are apprentices who learn from observing the Master at work. Theology should help them to better understand what they are observing and to follow his example.

A second methodological issue has to do with what Grant Osborne calls my "disjunctive thinking," i.e., "either/or" categories. Certainly Grant has a valid concern in principle. We all agree, I think, that we are dealing with divine mysteries that can only be described from differing perspectives which may be paradoxical. However, the paradox has no virtue in itself. Our "both/and" paradoxes may in fact simply hide sloppy thinking, and we ought to try to eliminate them in so far as they are the result of our own definitions. This calls for "disjunctive thinking."

Osborne's reference to my contrast of a "vicarious identification" with us in our shame and a "penal substitution" for our guilt provides a good test case to examine. So long as these remain only relative metaphors we can allow them to lie side by side. But when we begin to develop them into theological theory we need to note contradictory or conflictual elements, and assign priorities of classification and definition. The hermeneutics of inerrancy too often tends to gloss over distinctive differences in the texts in favor of a homogenized doctrinal meaning. Unfortunately this often missed the distinctive contribution of Scripture in its original context.

My contention is that the penal metaphor based on legal definitions of guilt should not be the primary basis upon which to construct a theory of atonement. Rather shame and vicarious identification provide the basic paradigm for a theological interpretation of the New Testament teachings. This does not mean that guilt is excluded (see pp. 223ff.), but gives it less priority. I am pointing out this methodological difference because it is a major difference in the approaches of biblical and systematic theology.

A third methodological concern involves the way in which we theologize about the preexistence of Jesus. John Hesselink, C. J.

Dyck, and Grant Osborne all commented on this in one way or another. Dyck wonders whether we can avoid the old heresies of subordinationism, etc., if we do not use the ontological categories of the Greeks. That is an interesting question, but one must ask in return whether the old heresies did not partially grow out of the inadequacies of the "Greek essence terms" in which they were couched. I think that in fact they did, and we need to check these categories by the biblical ones.

If the language of the biblical culture which refers to Jesus existing before his birth is to be understood formally as myth, then perhaps the demythologizing process of the early Greek theologians is the best hermeneutical procedure. If John 1:1 is already a clear hypostatization after the manner of Philo, the Jewish platonist, then we have an indication of next steps to be taken, at least in the Graeco-Roman context.

Following this lead, theologians attributed to the Logos a distinct ontological identity as "the Son." Then they identified the divine nature in Jesus with this "eternally begotten Son"--the "two natures in one person" dogma. Thus Jesus as "the Christ" might be said to be the pre-existent Son of God in as much as he is "one person" with the Son. In this way they translated mythical conceptions into rational ontological categories. *The Living Bible* reads this interpretation back into John 1:1 and paraphrases accordingly, "In the beginning was the Christ. . . ."

If, however, the biblical language is not mythical, and I think that it is not, then we need to follow another hermeneutical approach. The Old Testament writers freely personified God's attributes. They spoke of God's Wisdom, Word, Name, and Power as divine or angelic personifications. The question is whether such poetic personifications can properly be transmuted into a full hypostatization and, further, whether the language of John intends such hypostatization. Is the Christological terminology of the New Testament to be understood as a rational next step of attributing individual self-conscious identity to *"persona"* in the Godhead?

My own conclusion is that we do not have an adequate basis in the New Testament to confidently make this hermeneutical step normative. We can neither prescribe a universal dogma of Christ's eternal hypostatization as a *"persona,"* nor can we reject the validity of the Chalcedonian formula as a contextual statement. And I might add that even if we accept the language of Chalcedon, that does not resolve the modern question of how to understand a *persona*. The term did not mean an individual center of self-consciousness as it was used by the early church.

In my opinion this means that we must remain reverently

agnostic in the face of the mystery of Christ's preexistence as "the Word." To paraphrase the words of St. Augustine concerning the Trinity, we do not say "'co-eternal subsistence with the Father' in order to say something, but only to keep from being silent." At a later point I want to try to state what I think we can say with confidence about the preexistence of the Logos.

My treatment of the virgin birth accounts involves a similar methodological problem. Dorothy Jean Weaver faults me for two mistakes. First, I do not recognize that the biblical accounts of creation and virgin birth are "the best informed 'science' of the day." And second, at least by implication, she suggests that I do not find the proper dynamic equivalent to translate this "literal" scientific concept into our contemporary situation.

I would argue that before the modern period we can only speak of mythical, common sense, and even rational explanations as "prescientific." Neither in its linguistic mode nor intention is the creation account "scientific." Its author is a prophet, not a scientist, and his purpose and language are quite different from the language of science. His purpose is much nearer to that of Isaiah 40 than to scientific explanations, although I grant that the language of Genesis is more rational than some of the references to creation in the Psalms. On the other hand the virgin birth account, especially that portion which speaks of a Holy Spirit conception and Mary's response to the announcement, clearly has the characteristics of psalmody.

In any case the technicalities of this literary and linguistic analysis are the sphere of biblical scholars. My major concern is with Weaver's second question, namely, how we translate this prescientific language into contemporary theological explanations. This concerns the kind of linguistic mode we use in understanding miracles. Both creation and the new creation of the messiah are pictured as the miracle of God through the action of the Holy Spirit.

While miracles are experienced as part of historical experience, *miracle* is not strictly speaking an empirical category. It cannot function as a "literal" explanation for historical events. Rather, it is a way of understanding the real significance of mysterious and unusual historical events, whatever their scientific explanations may be. Miracles belong to the subjective-objective reality of historical experiences. Thus a mysterious event may occur within the natural chain of physical happenings, and yet be a miracle. (In his polemic against "counterfeit miracles" B. B. Warfield denied this.) In some cases science may be able to provide an explanation. In other cases an explanation may entirely elude us, but this has little to do with the event's miraculous character.

An example of a miraculous event which has both a scientific explanation and yet remains a miracle of God is the Exodus of Israel from Egypt. The account clearly speaks of a strong east wind blowing which dried the area for their escape (Exod. 14:21; cf. Josh. 4:23). This wind was seen as the instrument of the Lord, and the miraculous character of the account is heightened by the poetic language of water piled up on either side of the fleeing Israelites (Exod. 14:22). Compare the language of Psalm 77:16-20 and Isaiah 43:16-17 which are purely poetic accounts of the same miracle.

By way of contrast the creation and the resurrection of Jesus have no adequate scientific explanation at present. They can only be spoken of as the effect of God's "Word" which is certainly not to be understood as an audible verbal symbol (a literal explanation). The poetic language of Psalms 33:6-9 and 104:1-9 remains the proper language to speak of this miracle of creation. The words of Hebrews 11:3 will have to suffice.

The New Testament language of both the virgin birth and the resurrection is the language of miracle and has the same linguistic character as the Exodus and Psalmodic language. As I understand Luke 1-2, for example, the account speaks of historical experience and factual events, real people and places. This is not a mythical account. But at the same time it is not a simple empirical description of the historical experience. Like Exodus it is a theologically interpretative account which uses symbolic description to point to the real significance of what is occurring. Luke does not even attempt to answer our kinds of scientific questions, and to miss the symbolic dimensions of the story is simply to miss the rich, multiple dimensions of his meaning.

If this is true, then it is a mistake to insist that these accounts be translated into the literal scientific categories of modern western culture. Both Matthew and Luke affirm in their own way that the Holy Spirit of God was miraculously at work in the life of Jesus from his very conception. They do not give us a genetic explanation of how the infant Jesus was conceived. Rather, they leave us in adoration with the shepherds and wise men before the mystery.

Doctrinal Definitions

Three areas of doctrinal definition were questioned, namely, my treatment of "substitution" and the legal metaphor in atonement theory, some christological definitions that seem to throw doubt on an ontological concept of the Trinity, and concepts of Christ's identification with our humanity that might imply his sinfulness. Let me deal with these in this order.

Use of the Legal Metaphor. The concept of substitution is quite rightly applied to Christ's mission and ministry in our behalf. He died as a vicarious sacrifice and as our representative substitute according to the New Testament writers' understanding. But the concept of substitution is a broad one, and we must inquire in what sense he substitutes for us. That is my concern.

In post-Reformation orthodoxy the substitution was defined predominantly in legalistic terms. Christ died as a "penal" substitute. He bore the legal penalty for our sins by suffering the punishment of an undeserved death and the pangs of hell. Thus he satisfied the *retributive* justice of God by paying our debt to God's justice. He vindicated God's justice in the act of justifying the unjust.

In light of references to my rejection of the "Anselmic" concept of substitution, I must point out in the first place that this legal restatement of the Anselmic theory moves beyond Anselm's concept of "satisfaction" and the debt we owe to God. Anselm developed his theory in the context of the medieval feudal system of covenants, rights, and duties which masters and serfs owed to each other. The primary problem posed by human sin was the defamation of God's *honor* in the failure of his creatures to fulfill covenant obligations. Sin creates a "debt of honor" rather than a "debt to justice." This is more a matter of loyalty and shame than of legal guilt, although both are involved. The metaphor has to do with hierarchical rights rather than juridical punishment, whereas the post-Reformation theory is strictly juridical. This has clear implications for how we spell out the concepts of justification and substitution.

Perhaps in my zeal to dislodge the centrality of the legal metaphor I was too "disjunctive." The problem is not with Paul who obviously uses the legal metaphor, albeit in a rabbinic setting which had covenant law, not Roman justice, as its contextual metaphor. The problem is with post-Reformation interpretations of Paul. The concept of a "debt" of obedience or righteousness which we owe to God was transmuted into a "debt to justice" which Christ's substitutionary death paid. The "wages of sin" were spelled out as retribution and vengeance. Penalty became a legally assigned punishment. In short, the consequences of sin were spelled out in extrinsic legal, retributive terms rather than as intrinsic, moral consequences of sin.

The biblical concept of Jesus' substitution or vicarious action in our behalf begins with his identification with us and his willingness as our representative to suffer the consequences of human sin. In order to be our savior Jesus suffered death not for his own sin but because of his identification with us in our sin. He became the "scapegoat" for us. In this sense he died in our place. But the primary metaphorical context for this kind of language is the sacrificial altar and not the court room. And again, this has clear implications of conceptualizing the atonement in a shame oriented culture.

In contrast to the rabbinic concept that a person's death atones for the transgressions of his or her life, Paul insists that it is Christ's death on the cross (his blood) that makes atonement (Rom. 5:9-11). Thus, as I try to point out in the footnote on page 183, the phrase "justified by his blood" does not per se denote a theory of penal atonement. Rather the emphasis is on his death not ours.

Through Christ's identification with us in our shame, dying as our representative or substitute--the righteous for the unrighteous, the innocent for the guilty--we find reconciliation with God. Our guilt is forgiven (justification), and we are given a new lease on life. Justification is one of the important metaphors which Paul uses to help us understand how we have been freed from the consequences of sin. It is when this metaphorical language is translated into a forensic theory and then made the normative and controlling dogma of atonement that it becomes problematic.

Perhaps this is the place to comment on Dorothy Jean Weaver's criticism that my Gestalt of Jesus disregards the more judgmental aspects contained in both the parables and apocalyptic materials of the Gospels.

There is undoubtedly an element of judgment in the portrait of Jesus in the Gospels, and I have no wish to deny or diminish its seriousness. The judgment of divine agape against evil is inexorable. Agape is not indulgence. However agape operates with a different standard of judgment. It judges according to the *intrinsic* consequences of the act and not according to *extrinsic* legal codes.

It seems to me that the series of references which Weaver has included to substantiate her criticism illustrate my point. They are parables from organic life--good and bad fish, tares and wheat, the tree judged by its fruit, goats and sheep--not legislative or juridical metaphors. Other references speak of judgment as final alienation ("outer darkness"), no forgiveness as the final consequences of spiritual perversity (blasphemy of the Spirit), the inevitable consequences of an unforgiving spirit, etc. Indeed these examples are summed up in the words of Matthew 16:27, that the Son of man will reward everyone according to their works. This is the principle that one reaps what one has sown (Gal. 6:7).

By contrast legal punishments are largely extrinsic. That is, they are more or less arbitrarily prescribed penalties to facilitate political control. For example, a fine or prison sentence may be the prescribed punishment for speeding or drunk driving. My point is that God's law (Torah) is not a legislative document attempting to control the political situation. It is rather a constitutional mandate spelling out the basic nature of the human social order. It is a "covenant law," and the consequences of breaking it are certain and severe. "God is not mocked."

But God's judgment or sentence against evil is intrinsic. That is, it is simply a pronouncement of the consequences which are intrinsic in anti-God and anti-human acts. Selfishness breeds hostility. Violence begets violence. Dishonoring parents disrupts the whole social order. Breaking trust, i.e., deception, causes alienation. Idolatry debases the human self-image. These are real "judgments" on sin, and they are the "Law of God." But such judgment is not revenge or punishment in the sense of a vindicative legal penalty.

Clearly Jesus' life and teaching reflect this kind of covenant law. In the words of John 3:19, "This is the judgment [crisis], that the light has come into the world, and people loved darkness rather than light." On the cross Jesus accepted these consequences of human sinfulness in order to be our savior, and he died as our representative substitute. But this is not the kind of law and punishment appealed to by the penal substitutionary theory. Its controlling metaphor is legislative and juridical. It has often led to self-contradictory concepts of God's love and justice under its both/and rubric.

The Mystery of Trinity. The Christian doctrine of the threefold being of God grows in the first instance out of the experience and conviction that Jesus participated in the very self-identity of God. The personal intimacy and shared identity of the "Son" with the "Father" is the root of the doctrine (Matt. 11:27, John 10:14-15). The further experience of the Holy Spirit which was identified in the church as the Spirit of God or Christ gives rise to a triune rather than a binary formula.

The metaphysical existence of such a divine Trinity is a rational conclusion drawn from this faith experience and conviction. Trinitarian doctrine was not formulated as an analytical explanation or even as a description of God's essence. Rather, it was an attempt to give witness *in the philosophical thought forms of the time* to the church's experience of God in Christ through the Holy Spirit. As such it remains a mystery which, in the words of Augustine, is more to be adored and worshiped than understood and explained.

The mystery of Trinity, then, is grounded in the historical self-revelation of God, and is primarily a confession that God has revealed himself in a trinitarian mode. However, and this is part of the mystery, we must also say that the incarnation is only the historical revelation of God's eternal threefold personal being. God's own being was not perfected in his relation to Jesus but only reflected in it. The Christian confession is that God is the eternal Trinity.

Insofar as we are attempting to say anything about God's essential being, the doctrine of Trinity recognizes that God is essentially *personal* being. We do not fully understand the nature of our own personal existence, much less God's. However we do know that personal life is shared life. "Objects" become "subjects" in the intimate relation of participating in and sharing with other persons. A living being becomes personal in the existential recognition of another person over against itself. That is, personal being as we know it is by definition social being.

In the doctrine of the Trinity we are simply affirming that in God this social dimension called personal has existed from eternity. God did not *become* personal by creating creatures with potential for personal relationship. "In the beginning" God already was the personal God communicating in love. Neither did God become a Trinity in his self-revelation in Jesus. The creation itself is an act of personal communication--the "Word" (cf. Col. 1:15-17, John 1:2). God created other beings who potentially might share in his own multifold personal existence, but his own personal being does not depend upon that relationship.

Incarnation, Preexistence and Trinity. God endowed humans with the potential for personhood in relationship with himself. That is the meaning of our being created "in the image of God." Thus in creation the stage was set for an ever increasing self-revelation which draws humankind into personal communication and participation in God's own personal existence. In Scripture this is spoken of as God's being in covenant with his people.

In the incarnation this covenant or personal relationship of God to humanity is fulfilled not by human achievement but by God's own gift of himself. The potential of creation for full personal self-identity with God was at last realized in Christ. In him the "grace and truth" of God's full personal being was reflected in a communion of being that John describes as the "embodiment of the Word" (1:14). As Paul put it, we see the "glory of God in the face of Jesus Christ" (2 Cor. 4:6).

If we view the incarnation from the human side, we must speak of Jesus "becoming" the full personal image of God. In infancy he was not a fully developed person, just as we are not. Thus in his cradle he was not the embodiment of God in the same sense as when he hung upon the cross or was raised from dead. On the other hand, when we view his whole life from a post-resurrection perspective, we cannot speak of a time such as baptism or crucifixion or even resurrection when he began to be the "Son" (i.e., adoptionism). The *ex post facto* assessment must be that from his birth this one was destined to be "the holy Son of God" by virtue of the Holy Spirit's power which already overshadowed his conception.

My use of these categories of personal development led one participant to ask whether deity consisted in Christ's identifying with and living out the character of God, or first of all and primarily the embodiment of a preexistent divine substance (Edward Stoltzfus). Can his deity be spoken of in more than relational categories? Or to slightly rephrase the question, is there anything unique in the essential self of Jesus that might be called divine apart from his emerging self-identity with God?

It will be apparent from what I have said above that I hesitate to use the language of a pre-existent divine substance that indwelt the human Jesus. However, I do put more meaning in the word "self" than empirical psychologists do. Self is more than a relational construct. True, we come to know it in the unique relationships of ourselves with other selves. But the concept of selfhood points to a potential for responsibility, ego-transcendence, and recognition of other selves that makes the relationships possible. It points to a meta-empirical dimension of our being which I would call the *essential self*. It points to a *meta-psychical* dimension of our being like the word spirit points to a *metaphysical* dimension of reality.

What I have suggested is that we try to understand the "deity" of Christ in essentially the same manner that we understand his "humanity." That is, that we use a consistent personal analogy. His humanity is perceived through the character of personal relationships which he forms with other human beings. His deity is perceived through the character of his relationship to God. This does not mean that his deity can be reduced to a set of relationships any more than his humanity. In his essential self-identity he was one with God. One can, it seems to me, properly speak of his essential unity with God as the Son of the Father, but this is to be understood in personal rather than substantial terms.

Whether we conceptualize God's selfhood as a divine *living substance* or as a divine *personal being* which expresses itself in loving relationships that create selfhood, we are working at a fairly abstract and sophisticated level. I find it very difficult to conceptualize God's personal essence as a divine substance. What I am suggesting is that trinitarian personhood is best understood as God's essential nature and power to create beings "in his own image," i.e., to love. The distinct hallmark of love is its power to bestow personhood upon that which it creates. And therefore that we should recognize deity in Christ as the unique participation of Jesus in this personal essence of God.

If we view the incarnation from the side of the divine initiative we must say that God did not then begin to be a fully personal Deity at the time of incarnation. In the embodiment in Jesus God shared the fullness of his selfhood with us. Further, we must say that this is not the first manifestation of this same personal Deity. The word spoken at creation is the same Word spoken in Jesus, and that word, "Let there be light!" is an essential expression of the redeemer-creator God.

The concern to affirm the eternality of God *as he reveals himself in Christ* lies back of the concept of the preexistence of Christ. The Word of God which was fully expressed in Jesus was already in existence "in the beginning." This personal expression (Word), which is identified by John as both God's creative power and as his dynamic personal self-communication, was already the very essence of God "in the beginning." In other words, the doctrine of the preexistence of Christ attempts on the one hand to affirm the eternality of the trinitarian Godhead, and on the other to certify the authenticity of the self-revelation of that personal Deity in the Christ.

We cannot, however, speak of the individual, Jesus of Nazareth, as preexistent. Certainly Jesus did not mean to be taken literally as the Jewish leaders did when he said, "Before Abraham was I am." What the Orthodox doctrine intended to say is that the Word, which was equated with the second *persona* of the Trinity, existed before the incarnation.

Thus to be more precise I think that we may say with John that the "Word" has eternal existence. The identical, personal expression of God which was embodied in Jesus existed before the birth of Jesus, in fact, before the creation of the world. In the more traditional trinitarian language of the creeds, the *one* God whom we designate as "Father, Son and Holy Spirit" has always existed in this threefold personal manner. From this point, however, I am reticent to speculate about the ontological dimensions of God's being.

One final note on this subject: I am finding that even among our pastors we cannot take it for granted that the orthodox meaning of the word "person" as used in the "three persons of the Trinity" is understood. There is an understandable, but misleading tendency to give it a distinctly modern, individualized meaning, and to interpret trinitarian language as three individual centers of self-consciousness bound in the perfect agreement of love, will, and power. Thus we have moved far over toward the Antiochian, or "social trinity" end of the spectrum.

Christ's Sinlessness. A variety of tests have been proposed to determine whether one's view of Christ allows for his full humanity. For example, can you think of him as married and raising children? Now Mel Schmidt proposes the test of bad breath and dandruff. I personally have no problem imagining either one of these, but I doubt whether they are the real test. That test I have called "vulnerability." I remember through the years hearing all kinds of explanations of how Jesus could really be tempted without the real possibility of his failure. I think this anxiety explains why the docetic tendency has been so strong.

The doctrine of the sinlessness of Christ has been complicated by the Augustinian definition of "original sin." According to this definition humans have biologically inherited from Adam both a corrupt will that is powerless to resist sin, and "original guilt," i.e., the inherited debt or penalty of Adam's sin. When sin was defined in this way, it seemed imperative to absolve Jesus of such sin. Thus the doctrines of Mary's immaculate conception as well as that of Jesus.

I have suggested that the better solution to this problem is a redefinition of "original sin." When that is done, I see no reason why we should not follow the New Testament example of admitting that Jesus shared humanity's existential handicap but not its actual sinful failure to submit to the will of God.

Both the word "vulnerability" and the phrase "existential handicap" say the same thing. C. J. Dyck asks if the word vulnerable implies more than "the classical belief . . . that Jesus could sin but did not?" I see no basic difference. But it does underscore his identity with us and his lack of any advantage in overcoming temptation. I think that on the day of judgment no one will be able to look Christ, the judge, in the eye and say, "It is not fair. You had an advantage."

Theology and the creedal tradition

The relation of my theology to the creedal traditions of the church was raised in two ways. C. J. Dyck laments that I "go from the New Testament to the rationalism of the nineteenth century" with only a brief nod to the earlier theological tradition, and he expresses "an uneasy feeling of loss." At a later point in his critique it becomes clear that what he misses are the metaphysical categories of the Greek theologians. I can understand his concern as a historian, but must confess my surprise at this criticism. I was writing a one volume systematic Christology. Further, my major concern is with the orthodox tradition, not nineteenth-century rationalism.

I consider both post-Reformation Orthodoxy's theological

definitions and liberalism's restatements unsatisfactory for the same
basic reason. Both are governed by the fundamental postulates of
Aristotelian rationalism. The formulation of the issues, the logical
presuppositions, the terminology and categories of argument are
dominated by Greek metaphysical modes whether in their affirmation (Orthodoxy) or in their negation (liberalism). My own conviction is that Karl Barth did us a great favor when he challenged this
strangling control of the older rationalistic assumptions and pointed
us back to "the strange new world within the Bible." While we do
not necessarily follow Barth in every revision, certainly Oosterbaan
was correct when he said that Barth corrected Lutheran and
Reformed theology "along Anabaptist lines."

John Hesselink's challenge is at another level. He uses the contextual norm of Nicea-Chalcedon to critique my recontextualization
of the biblical material. I have challenged the orthodox view that
these fourth- and fifth- century statements fully and normatively
interpret the original meaning of Scripture for all times and places
so that thereafter Scripture should be read and interpreted according to the modalities of these ecumenical formulae. He accuses me
of a "reductionist Christology" on the grounds that it does not
measure up to Chalcedon.

But the question, as I see it, is whether my categories are faithful to the vintage New Testament Scripture in its first-century context. If Cullmann is right when he says that the New Testament
clearly calls Jesus the "Son of God," although not in the Chalcedonian sense, and I think that he is, then the crucial question is not
whether one's theology agrees with Nicea-Chalcedon, but whether it
is faithful to the biblical context and meaning. This was the Anabaptists' concern.

The criterion for orthodoxy in the fourth century and thereafter
was that one must affirm the authority of the universal tradition.
"Universal" was defined as that which had been believed "everywhere, always, by all." The decisions of the "ecumenical" councils
were by definition universal in space, and were enforced by imperial
edict. Also according to the rubric of universality the councils' decisions officially determined the meaning of the original writings--what
had always been believed. Today in a more historically conscious
time this appears to be a flagrant example of reading back into the
original records the theological conclusions of the fourth- and fifth-
century councils.

My contention is that while the formulae of the early ecumenical councils were faithful contextualizations for the cultural and
political situations of their own centuries, their interpretations do
not provide a universal authority which displaces the original norm.

They are valuable guides for continuing theological restatements, but they are not "infallible dogma" even in their original intended meaning, much less in the variety of interpretations now given them!

Luther, Calvin, and their followers questioned much of the medieval church tradition, but they did not question the normative authority of Nicea-Chalcedon as the interpretative grid for Scripture. They only added their own official creeds to them as authentic expressions. The assumed function of creeds and confessions in the classical Protestant tradition remained the same. Even in modern fundamentalism, which claims to be strictly "biblical," the normativeness of ecumenical creeds remains the covert assumption.

For example, the professors at "old" Princeton Seminary were required to sign the Westminster Confession of Faith and to take an oath to teach according to its formulae. At his inauguration B. B. Warfield declared that in his teaching "the system taught in these symbols [Westminster Confession] is the system which [would] be drawn out of the Scriptures." Then he added that this was so "not because commencing with that system the Scriptures can be made to teach it, but because commencing with Scriptures I cannot make them teach anything else."

My contention is that hermeneutically we must approach the biblical text in the first instance as a first-century contextual expression. It must be read against the background of the Hebrew Scriptures and the apocryphal and rabbinic literature of the centuries immediately preceding the New Testament. Theology, especially in the missionary context, must begin with this pre-Nicene New Testament as the basis of its contemporary contextualization. It simply will not do to read later contextualized interpretations back into the scriptural expressions as a normative grid for dogmatic interpretation.

This, as I understand it, was the concern of the original Anabaptists when they insisted on going back of Augustine, Chalcedon, Constantine and Nicea to the Bible. They did not reject these out of hand, but they refused to make them normative for the interpretation of Scripture. In this respect their rejection of a normative tradition was more radical than the magisterial reformers.

Contextualization. Finally, the whole question of crossing cultural borders with the Christian message is involved in relating traditional formulations to any new context. For me this becomes a major issue because I believe that today theology should be done in a missionary context. This does not mean that we can or should attempt to write an international theology. Rather, it means that we should consciously write contextual theology, i.e., theology for a time and place, not universal theology. And second, in each context we should attempt to dialogue with the churches of other cultures. We should welcome the insights which their cultural perspectives can bring to us.

In this regard I would like to call attention to Fumitaka Matsuoka's sensitive discussion of this aspect of my theological endeavor. Coming from Japanese culture into western Christianity, he recognizes the delicate balance between proclamation and dialogue as one "learns to negotiate the boundary of otherness."

My engagement with Japanese culture, and more broadly with Asian culture, taught me the difficulties of truly entering into another culture. At the same time it greatly stimulated my theological imagination by refocusing questions and providing new perspectives from which to read the Bible. The most important new perspective for me came from my observation and experience of a shame oriented society.

John Hesselink, who also served the church as a missionary in Japan, has commented on my interpretation of shame and guilt and their application in atonement theory. In this connection he comments on my attempt to reinstate shame as a moral and theological category for understanding the substitutionary work of Christ. He refers to my discussion in chapter 12 as an "attempt to identify/equate shame and guilt" and criticizes me accordingly.

I was in fact surprised by his interpretation of my position. I certainly had no intention of equating them. Rather I describe both patterns of social and psychological response and argue that both should be recognized as serious moral and theological categories. I say explicitly that sin is experienced in both modes (p. 206), and that the cross must deal with both our shame and our guilt (p. 207). My concern is precisely that in Japanese culture (and increasingly in our secularized western culture) there is no sense of a holy God in whose presence the truly shameful (sin) is defined.

Missiologically my concern is that when we proclaim the gospel in Japan we accept shame as the primary (but not the only) moral sanction and contextualize the biblical message accordingly. This would mean emphasis upon a holy God who rightfully defines the true parameters of shame, and in whose presence we ought to feel the anxiety of shame. God's holiness should be defined, however, in terms of the self-revelation in Christ rather than law. We should define sin more in terms of alienation than crime; the cross as reconciliation more than justification; blood as a cleansing agent, not legal penalty; and Christ's vicarious work as a compassionate identification with us rather than a balancing of the scales of justice. In other words, we should shift the paradigm, not to exclude guilt or to confuse guilt with shame, but to make shame primary for the interpretation of Christ's work in Asian cultures where shame anxiety is the primary moral sanction.

Again, in closing I want to thank my interlocutors. In a very real sense one learns what one has written by seeing how it is being read. When I read back through my book with their comments in mind I find passages that need improvement so that they say clearly what I intended without saying things that I did not have in mind. In some other cases I would appeal to my reviewers to give me a more careful reading. But in every case their interaction has been both exhilarating and humbling, and I am certain that if and when the work is revised it will be a better book for this consultation.

APPENDIX: BOOK REVIEWS

Journal of Mennonite Studies, vol. 6, (1988).
Norman Kraus's book *Jesus Christ Our Lord*, merits the attention of serious students of theology and mission. The author has written his volume on christology out of a wealth of experience in Christian work in the United States, Asia and Australia. In fact, *Jesus Christ Our Lord* was born in the midst of a mission assignment in Asia and Australia (1980-1987) under the Mennonite Board of Missions.

Kraus' guiding purpose throughout the book is to present a peace theology, which he says "should be a cross and resurrection theology" (p. 17). Stated otherwise, a peace theology is centered firmly in the Christ-event in which God disclosed himself creatively and redemptively to humanity. In working out this "Christology from a disciple's perspective," the author divides his discussion in two major parts. The first deals with the identity of Jesus as Messiah, Son of God; the second with the mission of Jesus as Messiah of God.

The chief value of the book is in its uncompromising presentation of a contemporary Anabaptist understanding of the person and mission of Jesus Christ. Norman Kraus grounds his thought and argument in actual human experiences, not simply in human experience as an abstraction. His complaint against standard theologies is precisely that they tend to extrapolate ideas from the primary Christian sources and render them in elitist language of Anglo-American culture. By contrast, this book, while it is thoroughly conversant with some of the major Christian thinkers of Europe and America, is occasional, situational, practical. Its theological metaphors are exemplified from real human interest stories, particularly those of the Far East (e.g. pp. 117f.).

Even though the discussion does not carry a polemical tone, it soon becomes evident that the author is dissatisfied with the mode of language and thought in theology developed in the West by both Protestant and Catholic theologians. For him, the context of theology is the church and its missionary vocation (p. 34). While this approach marks a significant departure from what is generally considered to be the norm of theological discussion, it is not avowedly an Anabaptist version of liberation theology (pp. 28f). Nevertheless, Kraus, in seeking to present "a coherent theological portrait of Jesus," distinguishes himself from theoretical theologians in favor of a theology of praxis not unlike that of some of the theologies of liberation thus: "Does that mean we are going to speculate, theorize, and dogmatize about Jesus? Should we not be more concerned to *experience* Jesus as Christ, proclaim him as Savior, and follow him as Lord?...In a word, it is *theory in the service of practice*" (pp. 36f).

On the question of the identity of Jesus, Kraus acknowledges that the language of christology, including the language of Scripture, is restricted to metaphorical imagery. He investigates the various images of Jesus represented in the several titles (Son of God, Messiah, Word, Lamb, etc.) and descriptions attributed to Jesus by the post-Easter church and from them all seeks to construct a *Gestalt* understanding of the significance of Jesus for the Christian community in the world. Above all, Jesus was/is God's self-disclosure. His deep significance is in the character of his kingship as *agape*. God's self-disclosure in Jesus is simultaneously a "self-giving"; the incarnation is God's gift to humankind out of his nature, which is *agape*. What is important is not the substance of the personality of Jesus as Son of God (debated repeatedly throughout Christian history), but the action of God in raising the crucified Jesus to Lordship, thus opening up the way to participation in the divine life.

For Kraus "participation" should be a principal idea in our understanding of Christology. Too much emphasis has been given to the forensic idea of the justice of God and not enough to the idea of relationship, as in a parent-child relationship. Christology properly understood should deliver us from shame and guilt and lead us into solidarity with God through Christ, giving us self-worth because God gives himself to us. "God is justified by an incarnation which finds its consummation in the cross, and not by a legal transaction which took place on the cross" (p. 157). In working out his christology, Kraus has redefined meaningfully the Anabaptist understanding of discipleship (*Nachfolge Christi*). Participation in Christ, solidarity with Christ, means more than reading the narratives of Jesus' activity in the Gospels, more than obeying the injunctions of the Sermon on the Mount. It involves the Christian in a radically new life in the midst of the old, a new kind of existence epitomized in the cross of Christ.

One is hard pressed to think of ways to improve this volume. Perhaps the following points should be considered. If the book should be revised some day, the note in the preface (p. 19) about the unavailability of sources should be deleted and the sources found and cited. Again, Norman Kraus sustained his thesis with flashbacks and repetition, but the repetitiveness at times intruded on the development of the argument. Furthermore, less headings and subheadings would enhance the flow of thought throughout the book. And while this author is to be commended for his diligence in handling the text of the New Testament, he seemed not to be acquainted with some of the outstanding New Testament scholars of our time. One in particular, E. P. Sanders, would have given substantial support to his thesis on participation in Christ. Kraus did cite the well known New Testament scholar, W. D. Davies, except that he misspelled his name at every citation (even in the bibliography) as, "Davis."

Despite these few criticisms, this book is praiseworthy and should be studied by Christians concerned for themselves, their families and the world.

V. George Shillington
Mennonite Brethren Bible College
Winnipeg, Manitoba

Mennonite Life, Vol 44, No. 1.

This work of systematic theology promises to make a major contribution not only to Mennonite thought but to all Christian understanding. It displays Kraus's many years of reflection on the issues, first as professor of religion at Goshen College and more recently as teacher in Japan for much of the past seven years. This review will focus on the book primarily in the context of Mennonite theology.

Since Mennonites began interacting with and learning from American culture at the end of the nineteenth century--an event which recent Mennonite historians have come to call the Quickening--an important and ongoing part of that dialogue has focused on theology. One can perhaps represent that conversation in terms of the often-used T. Traditional Mennonite thought (oriented by emphases such as discipleship, communitarian ecclesiology, peace, biblical authority, and concern for a lived-out faith), occupying the stem of the T, confronts a number of options along a continuum which occupies the cross bar of the T. In the 1920s this continuum stretched rather tightly between fundamentalist and liberal theology, but has always included a variety of experiential and philosophical options. The challenge for Mennonite thinkers was one of learning from the spectrum of options while maintaining a sense of Mennonite orientation and avoiding absorption into the spectrum. These interactions produced a variety of results and even those which maintained a Mennonite identity were not always particularly successful. For example, the era of Daniel Kauffman accepted much of fundamentalism's outlook and outline and then added a subsection to the outline--called 'restrictions'--in which to put the Mennonite emphases. On the other end of the Mennonite theological spectrum, concern for a lived faith turned into little more than declarations of tolerance and support for the liberal American political agenda.

Kraus' theology belongs to a different genre of Mennonite thought. It succeeds quite well at the task of dialogue with the major theological options--crossing the bar of the T--learning in the process, but continuing in a direction which is oriented by and reflective of the Mennonite, believers' church heritage. It is perhaps the first attempt in this century to articulate a comprehensive christology from a specifically Anabaptist, Mennonite, believers' church perspective.

Anabaptist, believers' church assumptions clearly orient this statement of christology. It is a peace theology, showing clearly that the cross and resurrection is God's way of dealing with evil. It makes Jesus himself, and "neither creation, general revelation, nor even special revelation prior to Jesus" the normative criterion for theology. And it accepts the New Testament witness as the authoritative source to Jesus, and the "composite apostolic witness...of the crucified and risen Lord" (pp. 17-18) as the shape of that theological norm. As the subtitle of the book indicates, these points work with the assumption that the Jesus so described will be one which Christians follow and that his story will be one in which they participate.

The methodological orientation of the book is that of narrative theology, made familiar to Mennonite readers by names such as John H. Yoder and Stanley Hauerwas. George A. Lindbeck and others have described the theoretical basis of this approach.

The book also addresses questions raised about christology and soteriology by the current generation of theologians. It assumes that the gospel has social as well as individual connotations. It speaks to questions raised in critique of the traditional Nicene-Chalcedonian definitions. Two such crucial questions are traditional orthodoxy's separation of christology from ethics and its separation of christology and atonement.

The book is divided into two major parts, the first dealing with who Jesus is and the second asking what his mission was. Part one stresses the genuine humanity of Jesus and explains how that humanity is the norm for defining authentic human existence. The discussion of the deity of Jesus then focuses on how this genuine humanity is the particular self-revelation of God in the world, so that in the life, death and resurrection of Jesus, God is present in the world. Kraus used the analogy of person to speak to Jesus' relationship to God. Thus it is God's identity which Jesus shares with us rather than written prophecy, doctrines or commands.

Part two, on Jesus' mission in the world, shows that Jesus' identity comes from what he did, and thus reveals Kraus's clear understanding of the inseparable link between christology and soteriology. To depict Jesus' mission, Kraus chooses to focus on Jesus as king, who inaugurates a new kingdom, a new way to live in history. King Jesus creates peace and justice, not by reforming the old institutions but by inaugurating a new movement. This kingdom is ruled by Apage. In Kraus's treatment, the cross--the supreme act of God's loving involvement in creation--answers the question of theodicy. It reveals humanity's act in opposing God as well as God's participation in the world and his way of overcoming evil. The resurrection which overcomes the consequences of sin--and not final judgment--is then seen as the ultimate justification of God in the world. After noting several biblical images of salvation, Kraus suggests that renewal of the image of God in humankind is the most appropriate metaphor of salvation. The concluding chapter of the book makes the point that salvation depends not on Jesus as a substitute for sinful humanity (which makes the mission of Jesus qualitatively different from that of his disciples) but on the repentant individual's solidarity with Christ, that is, on the creation of a new humanity which shares the mind of Christ and participates in his mission in the world.

A new and important contribution of the book is Kraus's distinction between shame and guilt. He rejects specifically the tendency of the western theological tradition to make escape from guilt and deserved penalty the primary problem of sin. Kraus separates shame from guilt, seeing shame as the primary element of atonement, a shame produced by awareness of the cross as God's way of confronting evil. Shame means a recognition that the sinner has unjustly offended God and others, and is thus aware of his or her true status, that of sinner. This recognition of sin then constitutes the first step of salvation, namely repentance or a desire to change brought on by the awareness of one's true state.

This approach to atonement and salvation in part plays off the motif of Abelard that the death of Christ does not cause God to change his mind but rather brings the sinful individual to an awareness of sin and the need for repentance. However, in contrast to Abelard, for Kraus salvation is not dependent on human response. He goes far beyond that motif in anchoring the work of Christ in history, incarnation and resurrection, with the cross as a bearing of humanity's sin and the objective proof of atonement located in the actual power of cross and resurrection to bring newness of life.

Undoubtedly the years Kraus spent in Japan contributed in a crucial way to his conceptualization of the book. That influence appears most clearly in the references to cultures which express the problem of evil in terms of shame rather than the western guilt orientation. That Japanese contribution appears explicitly, however, only in scattered paragraphs throughout the book. The theological argument of the book is comprehensible in its own right as a conversation with the received, western theological tradition.

This book dares to break new ground, both in its critique of the received theology and in its own statement of an alternative christology. As such an epoch-making work, some dialogue with it is to be expected. In fact not to engage in some conversation would be a dishonor and a disservice to it. In that spirit, then, I wish to make a few observations about this work whose direction and implications I can support unreservedly.

1) The discussion of shame as distinguished from guilt is significant and helpful. However, following the proper, strong emphasis on Jesus as king and on the corporate, social nature of the gospel (after all, a king has to rule over a kingdom), the treatment of shame takes place mostly in terms of the individual. Also appropriate would be development of corporate and institutional dimensions of the shame motif. Is it possible to deal with shame as a collective, for example when the church as an institution is caught up in a racist or economically exploitative society in spite of each individual Christian's intent to be non-racist and non-exploitative?

2) To pose the corporate issue in a different way, in my opinion Kraus could have made more of the ecclesiological dimension of christology. We use the name of Constantine to symbolize a shift in the conception of the church from a persecuted minority to an ally of the status quo. We still need analysis of the impact of the ecclesiological contribution to the shift from narrative to ontological categories, the separation of christology from atonement, and the separation of christology from ethics.

3) Kraus's critique of the various aspects of the Anselmian view of atonement is timely, appropriate, thorough and telling. In my opinion, however, Kraus has passed over too lightly the classic theory of atonement which has attained some prominence in revised and demythologized forms in several recent statements of Mennonite theology.

Only with great effort can one underestimate the significance of this book. It is must reading for all serious theologians, Mennonite or otherwise.

J. Denny Weaver
Bluffton College
Bluffton, Ohio

The Mennonite, vol. 103, no. 9.

In authentic Anabaptist tradition, C. Norman Kraus finds in
Jesus not only the key to interpreting the New Testament texts that
report on his life and mission but also the normative criterion for
understanding the entire biblical message. This christology from a
disciple's perspective is offered as "the introductory volume of a full
systematic theology" yet to come. We certainly applaud its
appearance and look forward to the publication of a second volume.

Written in a cross-cultural setting, *Jesus Christ Our Lord*
responds to two fundamental questions: Who is Jesus the Messiah?
And what is the mission of Jesus the Messiah? The approach of
traditional Protestant theologies (both conservative and liberal) has
been characterized by a largely rational methodology. In contrast,
the Anabaptists of the 16th century approached biblical interpretation from the perspective of the disciple community seeking to
undergird its life and work as the people of the Messiah.

While Kraus seeks to read the Bible from the perspective of an
Eastern culture (After all, the Bible is an eastern book!) and finds
new dimensions of meaning and application in the Scriptures, the
methodology and results are similar to those being experienced in
some of the Christian communities in Latin America. Living as they
do in social, economic and ideological situations similar to those that
characterized the New Testament milieu, the Bible provides a rich
source of guidance to these disciples in their suffering.

The recent recovery of Anabaptist vision, as it has been popu-
larized among Mennonites, has been largely historical and to a
certain extent ecclesiological in its focus. However, the implications
of this vision for our understanding of the meaning of the life and
death and resurrection of Jesus, as well as the mission of the Messianic community, have largely escaped us. This christology written
from discipleship, peace and missionary perspectives should help us
recover a more full-orbed biblical understanding of Christ and his
mission and that of his community.

Throughout the book the author offers examples of biblical
interpretation in a Believers' Church mode. In the final chapter he
describes the radical Anabaptist alternative for understanding and
experiencing Messianic salvation in terms of "solidarity with Christ."
This image stands in contrast to the traditional ways Catholics and
Protestants have perceived the experience of salvation as doctrinal

belief, incorporation into the body of Christ or imitation of Jesus. Undoubtedly all of these views include some measure of biblical truth. However, solidarity or *koinonia* with Christ is presented as the characteristic interpretative category for perceiving the experience of salvation in the Anabaptist tradition. This image is supported by a broad foundation of New Testament teaching.

But solidarity with Christ is not simply a powerful image for understanding the experience of salvation. It also defines our participation in Christ's mission. Here again the Anabaptist perception of its missionary vocation stands in marked contrast to traditional Protestantism. The witness of the Messianic community is seen as a representative continuation of Jesus' witness to the Father. This calls for "espousing the patience and purpose of Christ in servanthood." This will mean living a martyr existence under the sign of the cross. Our mission is the mission of Jesus the Messiah. Therefore the church dare not redefine mission in ways that justify recourse to violent power and allow it to escape martyrdom. We are saved and carry out our mission under the sign of the cross and in the hope of the resurrection in solidarity with Christ.

The author has written with admirable clarity on a theme systematic theologians have sometimes clouded with theoretical approaches and abstractions. However, it is not an easy book to read. It requires serious study (including the extensive footnotes, a mine of information and insights) if it is to be appropriated. And it may be that Christians of Eastern and Third World cultures will find this vision more understandable and more attractive than their counterparts within Christendom.

John Driver
Centro de Estudios
Montevideo, Uruguay

Conrad Grebel Review, vol. 6, No. 1 (Winter, 1988)

It is important and noteworthy that in present-day theological endeavors some attempt is being made to reflect theologically from other than European and North American contexts. It has become increasingly apparent of late that the dominant theology in the world today brings with it many presuppositions and elements which originated or gained their unique shape within that theological history which arose and developed in conjunction with Western civilization. It is also being recognized and to some extent regretted that in its missionary work the church of Europe and Asia did not and indeed could not always preach the "simple gospel," but often transmitted particular historical and cultural perspectives as well.

While it is not entirely clear just how this critique is to be taken seriously, one way to begin to rectify this situation is to hear and cherish the contributions of those theologians who speak from other contexts than our own. This is beginning to happen. Further help can be gained, although on a secondary level, from theologians who, although having their orientation in the Western world, nonetheless make a conscious and concerted effort to immerse themselves in non-Western cultures to reflect theologically from these other contexts.

In *Jesus Christ our Lord* the author makes a contribution in this latter way. Kraus, an American Mennonite who has recently lived for some time in Japan, draws on that experience to challenge certain longstanding assumptions of Western Christology. In conjunction with this contribution he also uses the opportunity to explore his longstanding conviction that "Anabaptist theology ought to be missionary theology" (Preface).

The book is divided into two major parts, the first dealing with the question: Who is Jesus? and the second with the question: What is the mission of Jesus? In the two opening chapters of the first part the author establishes the point that while a correct understanding of Jesus Christ must begin with personal and historical considerations, it must be maintained by faith and through historical analogy that "Jesus himself is the metaphor of God." This makes good sense not only for an interpretation of the New Testament but also for the Asian world of thought where the notion of the incarnation of divinity in a human agent is common. The Asian world would not be impressed with that interpretation of Jesus which emphasizes his humanity at the expense of his divinity.

In the remaining three chapters of the first part we find an extensive elucidation of the theme of Jesus as God's self-disclosure. In the author's view Jesus must be spoken of as the revelation of God in the sense that he is the fulfillment of God's intention for human life. It then follows that the perfection of Jesus is understood as Jesus' "perfect dependence as a fallible being (which does not mean 'sinner') upon the Father's infallibility." This is supported by a study of the signs in the gospels and in a discussion of various titles given to Jesus. The author concludes that the New Testament's language of embodiment speaks not of an ontological essence but of Jesus' identity with the self-revelation of God.

Kraus maintains that this line of thinking permits the believer to establish a relationship with God through Jesus within a framework of the analogy of person. He sees great advantage in this when speaking of Jesus in Asian cultures. While on the one hand there is the temptation by persons steeped in Asian religions to divinize

Jesus, making him into a nonpersonal docetic Christ, on the other hand the Asian mind is sometimes critical of the Christian religion for its tendency to reduce God to the level of human and self-centered (selfish) concern. The biblical interpretation offered by Kraus has the possibility of speaking to these concerns. The reader would have wished for more than only a page of reflections on this vital matter.

The second part of the book which deals with the mission of Jesus focuses especially on his kingly role. Kraus notes that the salvific work of Jesus is rarely understood as kingly work in traditional theology. And yet there is ample evidence in the New Testament for this connection. For example, the "kingdom of God" is synonymous with the "salvation of God." Salvation therefore includes the recognition of the lordship of Christ over the life of the believer.

Kraus then raises the crucial question: Why did Jesus have to die? His answer: The cross is the vindication of God's holiness in creation. That is, through the incarnation God accepts full responsibility for his creation and shows how he is at work in creation; namely, in compassionate love. This love is not compromised, but is carried through to the bitter end. To understand this we cannot use the legal or moral metaphors that have dominated the history of Christian thought. Kraus finds the personal metaphor more helpful. In Christ God shows himself to be altogether faithful to his own person, i.e., his own personal commitment to creation. The parent-child metaphor is helpful in expressing this faithfulness.

Among the various metaphors that have been used to express salvation, Kraus prefers those which suggest restoration such as the restoration of covenant relationship and restoration of the image of God in man. He finds this emphasis strongly supported in the Bible and in Anabaptism. The metaphor is not only immediate but also eschatological. That is, salvation is the completion in creation and humanity of what Christ has already begun.

In this reviewer's estimation the most significant contribution of Kraus comes with his discussion of the concepts of guilt and shame. He observes that while in Western theology preoccupation with guilt has dominated, Asians would understand the work of Christ more readily if the need to which soteriology speaks were cast not only in terms of guilt but also in terms of shame. He then shows that in the New Testament the concept of shame may well be central to an understanding of the need that reconciliation addresses.

This reviewer is not as positive about the final chapter of the book in which the author discusses the reception of salvation as our solidarity with Christ. The point that the work of Christ is not so much meant as a substitution for our work is well taken. But the author tends to overstate this point, claiming that "if what Jesus was and did are not *fully* paradigmatic and transferable to our life in the world and *ultimately* to the world itself, then his life has *only* the interest and value of a novelty" (italics mine).

This statement places an undue restriction upon Christ. It is not necessarily because Jesus Christ is fully and ultimately transferable to us and to the world that the identification can be built between him and us. Rather it is because he brings an inexhaustible and ever-renewing fountain of life to us and to the world that he can be one with us. Jesus Christ goes before us and exercises lordship above us. Otherwise we tend to reduce him to our best (but always limited) concepts. The tendency in Kraus's theology to do just that stems from his strong attachment to a theology of discipleship which at times overrides his Christology.

In his final discussion of solidarity with Christ Kraus becomes individualistic. One would have expected him to introduce the very important theme of the body of Christ--the church--here. Instead he says: "To participate in the mission (of Christ) one must share the style as a *disciple* calling all humankind to such a disciple style.... And what is true for the *individual* is also true for the world as a whole" (italics mine). Unfortunately the church is bypassed in this discussion.

Although the book is somewhat wide ranging and at times not clearly focused, Kraus has provided a valuable service to the theological community,and especially to those who are pursuing the Anabaptist-Mennonite discussion in theology. His main contribution is probably not in terms of providing an integrated Asian perspective for us. His relations relating to an Asian perspective are offered in scattered bits throughout the book. He does provide the theological community with some significant integrated ideas concerning the significance of the cross of Christ.

Helmut Harder
Canadian Mennonite Bible College
Winnipeg, Manitoba

The Mennonite Quarterly Review, Vol LXII, no. 4 (October, 1988).

This excellent book by a contemporary Mennonite theologian spells out in the thought patterns of modern cultures and languages a Christological alternative--only suggested by sixteenth-century Anabaptists--to Protestant reshaping of Augustinianism. In so doing, the author has himself moved away from thinking out of the context of traditional Western (Greek) metaphysics and into what he suggestively calls the realm of the metapersonal--more in line with

the ethos of modern social and psychological thought. He has read
Anabaptism from that perspective and reinterprets it as a provocative thesis, ordering his biblical and theological materials accordingly
and offering his careful reader not only many fertile seeds in
exegesis and interpretation, but also the ripened fruit of more than
thirty years of teaching in Mennonite colleges and seminaries.

What is the thesis? In classical Christological terminology
Kraus opposes Docetism with a strong insistence upon a human--
even fallible though not sinful--servant king who intends to be followed. Despite carefully nuanced interpretations, one might sense
that in so doing Kraus has moved close to an adoptionist position
which is scarcely sensitive to the concerns of classic Trinitarian doctrine. But his preoccupation is elsewhere--a Christ with whom it is
really possible for humans to be in solidarity through suffering love,
for that is salvation. It is a "Christology from below" as perceived by
a disciple's reading of the New Testament for guidance in a restored
and transformed life and community of faith rather than that of a
catechumen reading the ontological creeds' interpretation of the
New Testament as a foundation of belief.

A second major preoccupation of the author is to understand
the suffering love of King Jesus in other than classic Protestant (read
Anselmian) thought patterns of vicarious punishment, which he
rejects because they circumscribe divine love with punitive justice
according to the law of talion (retaliation), unworthy of God as
revealed in Jesus. And as a peace theologian the author draws a
clear connection between this understanding of atonement and Con-
stantinian models of peace and justice which contradict those found
in Jesus' life, teaching, suffering and resurrection. Kraus's own
understanding of the atonement grows, on the one hand, out of his
perception of the incarnation of the cross as divine response to
alienation and shame--in his judgment more biblical, more primary,
more profound and more closely related to interpersonal relations
than the more superficial guilt expressed in legal metaphors and
categories. Since most Western missionary effort has been condi-
tioned by centuries of acculturation to Roman law, his approach is
seen as a fresh cross-cultural contribution to missionary theology,
particularly in the shame-conscious Orient, where Kraus served as a
theology professor in India and Japan and where this book was first
written and given as lectures.

On the other hand, the author's understanding grows out of his
conviction that, after the cross, the resurrection--with its eschatological implications--must be seen as God's final word of love. From the
point of view of traditional orthodoxy this ignores post-resurrection
dimensions of the fulfilled Christ event, including a last just vindica-

tion and punitive judgment. This the author gains from a Jesus-oriented critique of a Jewish-Christian synthesis of apocalyptic and cross. Kraus recognizes that this new approach of the New Testament is not fully developed therein and that it leaves some questions unanswered. But from the third-world missionary perspective of this reviewer it is even more significant to observe that there is missing in Kraus's *Gestalt* of Jesus that important New Testament (and Gospels) dimension of one "seated at the right hand of God until all his enemies become his footstool" and who promises and sends the Holy Spirit of Power, which is indeed much more than just an attitude like that of Jesus. This reviewer's identification with those involved in living "history from below" (as did the early church) suggests that Kraus's slighting of eschatology and the Holy Spirit is a weakness both as missionary and as Anabaptist-inspired Christology. Yet one may no doubt anticipate a more developed modern expression of that New Testament and Anabaptist thrust in a further volume of theology promised by the author. Until then he has already made well the missiological point--challenged more and more in numerous theological circles--that authentic theology must begin with Christology, and one based on King Jesus of the Gospels, experienced by disciples. It was indeed the Anabaptist orientation.

David A. Shank
Blockhaus-Abidjan, Ivory Coast

Sword and Trumpet, Vol. LV, no. 4.

On the very last and unnumbered page of *Jesus Christ Our Lord: Christology From a Disciple's Perspective* (Scottdale, PA.: Herald Press, 1987, $19.95) a broadly smiling photograph of the author, C. Norman Kraus, Ph.D., appears. It is no laughing matter that this ordained preacher in the Mennonite Church with so many accomplishments to his credit should embrace the views which this book contains. But he appears to have the backing of the establishment.

On the first page of the book endorsements from two noted spokesmen appear. An adjunct professor of religion at Goshen College suggests that the book is "...a rigorous quest for biblical authenticity..." and the President and Professor of Theology at Goshen Biblical Seminary endorses this books as a "...creative Christological proposal...."

Reading this most recent book from Kraus will be no laughing matter for Mennonite believers who consider themselves in the stream of historic, evangelical, conservative Christianity, and who hold in high esteem the writings of Menno Simons, John Horsch or

John C. Wenger. It will not be funny for Mennonites who believe that the doctrines embodied in their historic statements of faith represent the truth "once delivered to the saints."

What will the state and fate of the Mennonite Church be, should the Christology advanced by Kraus become the standard dogma for the heirs of Menno? Just to think that Mennonite martyrs went to the stake rejoicing in the affirmations which this book undermines.

Jesus Christ Our Lord breaks new ground indeed, at least for Mennonites. Or is it a rehash of the age old criticism of the Bible "doctored up" with smooth words for unsuspecting people? Mennonite "thinkers" are growing more bold with each passing decade. We are witnessing a coming-out-of-the-closet of beliefs that only a few years ago would have been anathema in regular Mennonite circles. Mennonite theologian Gordon Kaufman produced his *Systematic Theology* out of Harvard University, but until now it would have been unthinkable for Herald Press to publish it. Such reluctance is certainly quickly giving way to a willingness to push far beyond the boundaries of a relatively recent past. Kraus' *Jesus Christ Our Lord* and Kaufman's *Systematic Theology* have so much in common that conservative, evangelical Christians have proper grounds for calling the denominational press to account for the publication of this book.

Reading *Jesus Christ Our Lord* is serious business. It is a man's job. Some preliminary observations are in order. *First*, the reader should know that Kraus has a constitutional bias against conservative theology. His writings have long been directed against fundamentalism and evangelicalism. Kraus is known as a harsh critic of creedal, orthodox Christianity. There is perhaps among American Mennonites no writer who excels Norman Kraus in undermining and undoing the basics of evangelical faith, unless it should be Kaufman.

It did not begin with the writing of this book. But this is likely considered his masterpiece.

Second, his experience in the Orient with its professed demand for developing a Christology for a mission setting provided yet an ingredient not a major factor in his previously published works. *Third*, Kraus is a thinker and an able writer. He is clever in his ability to question the truth and plant doubt without the undiscerning reader realizing it. Much of his unorthodoxy is clothed in indirect language and tucked away in footnotes where some of his worst error is to be found.

Fundamental to an understanding of the book is the author's low view of the Bible. He does not believe in the inerrancy of Scripture. Yet, he does cite the Bible repeatedly. His command of the biblical text is admirable, particularly for one who can relegate much of it to insignificance. He is not in the same class with Tillich, a "theologian" of the past generation who rarely referenced his comments with biblical quotations. Kraus' weakness is not his lack of biblical knowledge.

He parts company with historic Christianity in his insistence that rationalism has misdirected its conclusions. He maintains that the orthodox theologians relied over-much on Greek modes of thinking. To interpret the Bible with an eye to logical consistency is to miss its basic intent. The author is completely impatient with all who are in the reasoning orthodox camp.

He finds his company with those who understand the biblical text from what he calls a Hebrew perspective. That is, that Scripture is presented in the mode of picture, myth, allegory and poetry. One should not expect to find reasoned consistency, nor will all accounts harmonize. It should not be expected that the Bible will be picture-perfect. Scientific accuracy is not necessary. The biblical accounts are often on the order of sermonic illustrations, not literally true or empirically verifiable but are simply the bearers of a spiritual message all the same. Just as one does not squeeze the word pictures of poetry for scientific testing just so the informed reader will not try to compress biblical statements into logical structures. So believes our confused brother.

He seems to be caught in the jaws of a paradox. On the one hand he insists on throwing overboard reasoning interpretations of the Bible while on the other he himself adopts an explanation which sounds very rationalistic. The ordinary reader cannot help but be struck by the reasoning power and erudition which is displayed in the book. How, then, can the author claim for himself a place closer to an authentic understanding of the Scriptures? He does it on literary and historic grounds. He tries to make a case for understanding the Bible as did the people who wrote it at the first, whose mentality and thinking were Hebraic.

Who is there to come forward and pronounce Kraus wrong? The structures will not do it. Where are the so-called "church channels" to deal with such a situation? The order of the day seems to be one of SILENCE! Before God--who will answer?

Think again of the mass of Christians from the early centuries until now, including our Anabaptist forefathers and Mennonite believers, literalistic Christians from the Reformation until the present. Were they all wrong? The Anabaptist Reformation--was it all wrong in its view of Scripture and were the bulk of Mennonite theologians along with earnest Bible-believing saints all wrong? Only liberal academics and the intelligentsia will find much comfort in Kraus.

Taking leave of biblical inerrancy and logical consistency Kraus can look in the Gospels for a general *gestalt* (form) for Jesus. Individual statements which fail to conform to the *gestalt* may be ignored as unreliable or irrelevant. The Jesus who is derived from this process is pictured as a human person of extraordinary commitment to God. His virgin birth and pre-existence seem to be denied. The reader is left with a thoroughly human Christ whose general description and meaning may have more in common with the Jesus of the Jehovah's Witnesses than with the divine-human Son of God.

This is not intended to be a full scale critique of this book. There is more to be written. It is enough to say that in severing the moorings inherent in evangelical theology Kraus has cast himself and all who follow him upon the murky waters of theory, supposition, dubious interpretation, and suspicious exegesis. At the moment there is little likelihood that he will take many of the saints with him but his views will receive sympathetic hearing at the academic level. Eventually, they will be reflected by young seminary graduates and then later in the pew. The sad repetition of the fall of the Dutch Mennonites may be unfolding before our eyes in the United States, 100 years after the onset of the demise of the church in the Netherlands. At least this is the very route which the Dutch Mennonites took to their own destruction. It is no laughing matter. Read John Horsch's *Mennonites in Europe* for the full story.

A Crisis Among Mennonites in Christology is due and should be forthcoming soon including a more detailed review and critique of the Kraus book.

You will be hearing more from this reviewer and also from world famous evangelical theologian, Dr. Carl F. H. Henry who believes this book by Kraus is a vigorous attack on the historic evangelical view.

George R. Brunk II
Harrisonburg, Virginia

Gospel Herald, vol. 80, no. 46 (November 17, 1987) p. 803.

As a pastor I see myself as a mediator between the world of academic biblical or theological studies and the practical questions people wrestle with every day. To aid me in that task I want books that interact with the scholarly world but also give me pointers for practical application of scholarly insight. I find few such books. Most seem to stay largely in the scholarly world and speak mainly to other scholars, or to address practical questions without allowing the scholarly world to ask its helpful critical questions.

The subtitle of C. Norman Kraus' new book, *Christology from a Disciple's Perspective*, implies an attempt to bridge the gap, as do Kraus' prefatory comments that the book grew out of trying to theologize about Jesus in the context of missionary work in Japan. Kraus shares a Christology that has clearly been affected by conversation with the realm of critical scholarship, but one which also moves beyond that realm to ask how the issues he addresses might be relevant to the disciple's daily concerns.

Kraus' concerns include asking who Jesus is and what his mission was and is. As he works at answering those questions, Kraus interacts with a wide variety of possibilities, including those proposed by both liberal and orthodox Protestantism as well as more Eastern thought styles. He suggests that Protestantism has tended to produce rationalistic answers floating up in a sky of meta-physical abstractions. This has tended to "substitute theoretical justification of logical statements for an authentic practical response of the church to Jesus Christ as *Lord*." In Eastern contexts Jesus tends to become a symbol of a mystical oneness at the heart of the cosmos, which also tends to divorce Jesus from the flesh-and-blood reality of daily living. Kraus contrasts this with the Anabaptist concern for a lived theology embodied in the real world of historical forces.

This concern for a lived theology leads Kraus to suggest that the best way to understand the atoning work of Jesus is through personal metaphors rather than the more abstract legal or moral metaphors that often dominate in Protestant theology. An important personal metaphor for Kraus is that of parent-child. We are the children who, having sinned, are in broken relationship with God our parent. In Jesus we see what God's response to that brokenness is, and it is to offer a love willing even to die on a cross in order to break through our alienation and restore us to membership in God's family. From this restored position we are then called to reach out to the alienation of others through expressing our solidarity with them as Jesus demonstrated to us God's solidarity with us.

More than such a brief sketch can indicate, Kraus' book serves as a helpful summary of countless biblical, theological, and epistemological issues that must be dealt with in arriving at a solid Christology. He does a good job of pulling out of such complexity a Christology compatible with Anabaptist concerns for peace and an understanding of salvation that applies it to all levels of life in the world, not just a personal and private one. I will often turn to it as a reference work.

Kraus does frustrate me at points. For one, though he does begin to explore some of the implications of theologizing across cultural contexts, he could have done more, and I read his preface as promising more. For another, I found it difficult to pull out for review purposes thematic threads that could be made intelligible in a few words for a nonspecialist audience.

This is partly because Kraus does not, in the end, completely bridge the gap between academia and the disciple's world. He poses the "disciple's" perspective as an alternative to more abstract approaches to Christology, but manages to pull this off only at a relatively abstract level. At a few points he uses stories as helpful illustrations. He could have done this more. Since he didn't, the reader is left with a tremendous amount of work in moving from theory to application, from theology to discipleship.

Perhaps the promises I read into Kraus' subtitles and his preface were different ones than he intended to make. Or perhaps I am revealing only my own dense mind. In that case my frustrations are my problem, not his. And no matter whose problem they are, they do not destroy a good book.

Michael A. King
Germantown, Pennsylvania

CONTRIBUTORS

C. Norman Kraus, author of *Jesus Christ Our Lord: Christology from a Disciple's Perspective*, was long-time professor of religion at Goshen College, Goshen, IN. He and his wife Ruth, who now reside in Harrisonburg, VA, have also served in a number of overseas mission teaching assignments, most recently in Japan.

Dorothy Jean Weaver is assistant professor of New Testament at Eastern Mennonite Seminary, Harrisonburg, VA.

Grant R. Osborne is professor of New Testament at Trinity Evangelical Divinity School, Deerfield, IL.

Fumitaka Matsuoka is the academic dean at Bethany Theological Seminary, Oak Brook, IL.

Melvin D. Schmidt is the pastor of the First Mennonite Church, Bluffton, OH.

C. J. Dyck is professor of Anabaptist and Sixteenth Century studies at the Associated Mennonite Biblical Seminaries, Elkhart, IN.

I. John Hesselink is the Albertus C. Van Raalte Professor of Systematic theology at Western Theological Seminary (Reformed Church in America), Holland, MI. Hesselink formerly was president of Western Theological Seminary and a missionary to Japan.